LIVING A
CHOCOLATE LIFE

A Bible
Study
for Women

Living
a Chocolate Life

Savoring God's Sweet Grace

Deb Burma

CONCORDIA PUBLISHING HOUSE • SAINT LOUIS

To Cory: I am so blessed to share this chocolaty-rich life of God's sweet grace with you. Thank you for your support, encouragement, and love. Our Savior Jesus Christ is glorified through your life of faith and in your service to Him. To God be the glory!

Copyright © 2015 Concordia Publishing House
3558 S. Jefferson Avenue, St. Louis, MO 63118-3968
1-800-325-3040 · www.cph.org

Scripture quotations are from the ESV Bible® (The Holy Bible, English Standard Version®), copyright © 2001 by Crossway Bibles, a publishing ministry of Good News Publishers. Used by permission. All rights reserved.

Manufactured in the United States of America

3   4   5   6   7   8   9   10   11   12   25   24   23   22   21   20   19   18   17   16

Table of Contents

INTRODUCTION

Sweet. Rich. Satisfying. Chocolate—can you imagine life without it? I can't either. And we're not alone. I recently purchased a gift packet of hot chocolate with big bold words across the front reading, "I LOVE YOU EVEN MORE THAN CHOCOLATE!" The cashier studied the packet, looked at me, and sighed, "You can't give this to very many people, can you?" Her implication? There is little we love more than chocolate! If we cannot imagine life without it, does that mean we live "a chocolate life"? (Sounds yummy, doesn't it?!) But what does it *really* mean? For starters, living *a chocolate life* is about so much more than our favorite confection; and it's about a love that's incomparably greater too!

Living *a chocolate life* means sampling everything from bitter nuggets of pain to sweet morsels of joy. Some days are dark and lumpy; others are light and smooth. Whatever the shape, flavor, and texture of our days and however our lives are packaged, we can savor God's rich and *endless* supply of grace in Christ! Wrapping us in forgiveness, the Holy Spirit fills us with sweet faith in our Savior.

I invite you to choose your favorite chocolate treat, ask others to join you for something sweet, rich, and satisfying, and then sink your teeth into this uniquely chocolate-filled women's Bible study. We'll explore what it means to live *a chocolate life* in several ways. During each delicious session, we will look at our lives in light of God's grace.

Before you begin, you should know that every sumptuous session contains several special ingredients:

A CHOCOLATE SAMPLER

To start each session, check the boxes in a series of fun chocolate statements as they apply to you. (Many statements relate to the topic of the session, providing a sampler of what lies ahead.) This opportunity can help break the ice in a Bible study group and enable you to open up to one another in small ways, which will foster friendships, encourage communication, and open doors to share in larger, more significant ways throughout the study and beyond. Starting with the second session, *A Chocolate Sampler* will also provide an opportunity to share a tidbit from the previous one.

MEMORY MORSEL

Each session also begins with a theme verse, a morsel of Scripture, to commit to memory. I encourage you to write each week's verse on a card and display it in a prominent place where you'll see and recite it regularly. As a special incentive to memorize, try placing the verse card in a candy bowl with at least seven chocolate kisses (one or more per day). Each time you say the verse, grab a kiss! Begin each group study session with a *Memory Morsel* moment, tucked into that session's *Chocolate Sampler* as a reminder. Encourage one another to commit each morsel to memory, using this moment to recite the previous session's verse.

TAKE A BITE

Scattered throughout the study are brief questions asking you to "take a bite"—to pause and ponder a personal question. Whether you are studying *Living a Chocolate Life* alone or with a group, you'll benefit by first reading through a session on your own, pausing to *take a bite,* and slowly chewing on these brief questions for personal reflection. As you gather together, revisit these questions to share more deeply in group discussion.

DIG IN!

These numbered questions give you something to really sink your teeth into. You'll *dig in* to the study more deeply by reading Scripture, responding to questions, and applying them to your chocolate life. Allow time for rich and reflective discussion. Answers can be found in the "Answers to *Dig In!* Questions" at the back of the book. *Note:* Each session contains seven questions. You may complete a session in one sitting or savor it more slowly, *digging in* to one question each day for a weekly Bible study plan, then discuss the entire session as a group.

CHOCOLATE FUN FACT

In each session, you'll find a tidbit of chocolate history or trivia, shared as it applies to the topic of the session. It often aids in illustration!

PRAYER: SWEET SUPPLICATION

Included at the end of each session is a prayer, a *sweet supplication* to the Lord, as you wrap up each grace-filled *chocolate life* study. I encourage you to also open each study time with prayer, whether reading alone, preparing for group study, or as you are gathering with your group. Ask the Lord to guide and grow you through the Word, by the power of the Holy Spirit.

CHOCOLATE RECIPE

A rich chocolate recipe is included with each session, connected closely by theme and topic. As you make and bake, savor and serve each mouthwatering dessert, let it serve as a reminder that you live *a chocolate life* by the grace of God. Share a related nugget from God's Word with those who indulge beside you!

CHOCOTIVITY (CHOCOLATE GROUP ACTIVITY)

Each unique *chocotivity* is tied to the session's theme, serving as a tangible reminder of that topic and of our chocolate-rich life in Christ! These creative *chocotivities* provide an occasion to continue dialogue about each powerful topic with one other in your Bible study, while offering fun fellowship and a hands-on reason to bring even more women together. Several *chocotivities* result in the creation of gifts, tangible ways to share God's Word and His lavish grace with others. You may choose to have your *chocotivity* time immediately following or included with Bible study, or you may wish to set another place and time, especially if inviting others!

Are you ready for a treat? As you savor your first bite from this assortment of chocolate topics, it is my prayer that you will **"grow in the grace and knowledge of our Lord and Savior Jesus Christ,"** living a chocolate-rich life in Christ. **"To Him be the glory both now and to the day of eternity. Amen"** (2 Peter 3:18).

—Deb Burma, author

$\mathcal{S}$AVOR

A CHOCOLATE SAMPLER

Check all that apply to you, and then discuss as a group:

- ☑ *You have savored a rare, expensive European chocolate.*

- ☑ *You have survived a chocolate baking catastrophe.*

- ☑ *You often keep chocolate nearby to savor during Bible study or devotion time.*

- ☑ *Milk chocolate is your preference. Or dark. Or white. (Circle one. Or more.)*

- ☑ *You live a chocolate life as you savor God's sweet grace in Christ! (Intrigued? Read on!)*

MEMORY MORSEL

"In [Christ] we have redemption through His blood, the forgiveness of our trespasses, according to the riches of His grace, which He lavished upon us." Ephesians 1:7–8

savoring $\mathcal{G}$race

Imagine you are about to receive the most exquisite chocolate indulgence. Not your average grocery-store candy, not even a finer, specialty-shop variety, but an extremely rare, delicate chocolate made from the highest quality cacao beans found only in the most remote region of Africa and shipped to

CHOCOLATE FUN FACT
Cocoa butter, the fat naturally found in the cacao bean, melts just below body temperature, which is precisely why fine chocolate melts in your mouth so easily. (No wonder it disappears so quickly!)

⇨ **CHOCOTIVITY**
Chocolate-Savoring Taste Test! (Turn to the end of this session to read about it in detail. Consider including this special activity at this point during your study time.)

only one exclusive shop, where each delicacy is handmade. There is a price to pay for this most exclusive chocolate. And someone who loves you has gone to great lengths to find and purchase this delicacy from the finest chocolatier in the world.

Now your loved one is ready to give this precious gift to you. You hold out your cupped hands to receive this extravagant present. As you look down, your jaw drops! A rare, foil-wrapped delicacy lies in your hands, waiting to be gently opened. *Go ahead; unwrap it.* What will you do next? Will you pop the candy in your mouth, chew quickly, and swallow as soon as possible to get rid of it? Oh my, *no*! For a once-in-a-lifetime moment like this, move the delicacy slowly toward your mouth. Observe the beautiful color. Take in the rich aroma. Lay this pure chocolate perfection on your tongue and allow your taste buds to dance with joy as you *savor* this exquisite morsel. Hold its delicate richness on your tongue for as long as possible, taking in the indescribable flavor and the smooth, creamy texture. And then notice how, ever so slowly, the sumptuous treat melts, trickles down your throat, and disappears.

Finished. A memory. Fleeting, wasn't it? That's how it is with chocolate. And that's how it is with most precious things we savor. We hold onto them as long as we can.

We revel in joys and friendships of our school years only to part ways upon graduation. We delight in our children's youth; then, before we know it, the nest is empty. We treasure the time spent with a loved one who lives far away; then, all too soon, we say good-bye. We relish getaway moments and weekends of rest, when we receive respite from the routine pressures of life; and in the blink of an eye, Monday morning arrives again. We savor the best things of life as long as possible because, far too quickly, they disappear. Finished. A memory. Fleeting, weren't they?

As women *living a chocolate life*, we get to savor something so much greater than all the other things of life: we savor the gift of *God's sweet grace!* His sweet, saving grace is the one thing we can savor that will not melt, grow up, or leave. It will not change, fade with time, or disappear. God's Word assures us that grace is ours for much more than a fleeting moment; it does not become a mere memory but lasts for a lifetime.

So what exactly is grace? By definition, *grace* is "unmerited, undeserved favor." In our sin, we certainly don't deserve God's favor, do we? And there is nothing we can do to earn or merit it. But does God ever favor us! He is crazy about us! And what do we receive as a result?

Check this out: **"In [Christ] we have redemption through His blood, the forgiveness of our trespasses, according to the riches of His grace, which He lavished upon us" (Ephesians 1:7–8).**

#1 dig in!

Ephesians 1:7–8 above (this session's *Memory Morsel*) is full of good stuff. It proclaims clearly what we receive by God's grace and how He accomplished that for us. Explain here in your own words:

a. What is meant by the word "redemption"? How does this powerful word help to further define the forgiveness that we receive through Christ for our "trespasses" (sins)?

b. What does it mean to "lavish" something upon someone? (Think of a chocolaty example.) What is being lavished here? What does this say about the measure of our Savior's loving mercy toward us?

Earlier we talked about the best things of life, the things that we savor. By far, grace is the best *thing* of life. **"For by grace you have been saved through faith. And this is not your own doing; it is the gift of God" (Ephesians 2:8).** Grace is the best gift we will ever receive, even finer and richer and more extravagant than the most exquisite chocolate!

#2 *dig in!*

Open your Bible to **Ephesians 2:4–9** and read the context that surrounds the grace-filled words of **verse 8**, telling us of God's free gift of salvation that is ours by grace through faith. Write down the words that speak of God's demeanor toward us and His actions on our behalf:

✂ TAKE A BITE

Have you ever felt that your sins outweigh the size of God's grace? that your mess has spread beyond the reaches of His mercy? Perhaps you keep falling into the same sinful trap and have begun to wonder how you can possibly be forgiven. Ponder this, but don't stop here! Read on . . .

Every fleeting moment and all the other valued things of life are also gifts from God to enjoy. Empowered by the Holy Spirit, we can savor our many blessings, giving thanks to the Lord for them while continually savoring His rich, lavish grace, His unending mercy, and His promised salvation in Christ.

While it's difficult to grasp the extent of God's grace, to comprehend how great is His love, how rich is His mercy, how generously He lavishes His grace upon us, we have His Word on it! These things are ours, although we've done nothing—and can do nothing—to deserve them. Maybe you've heard only the Law. The shame of your sins rings loud in your ears, condemns you, and reminds you that you do not deserve forgiveness. Maybe others have attempted to place conditions on God's grace, causing you to wonder if you've sinned beyond the reaches of His mercy. As a result, maybe you find yourself falling into faulty thinking: *Yes . . . but you don't know what I've done. I continue to fall in the same sinful traps. You wouldn't believe how badly I've messed up.*

Chocolate-Frosted Grace

Let me tell you a story about mess-ups. One day I was expecting guests, and I planned to create a special dessert of unparalleled quality—a rich, extravagant, three-layer chocolate cake. (The recipe is included at the end of this session.) The made-from-scratch batter rose beautifully in my round layer cake pans as it baked and filled the house with a chocolaty aroma.

Fresh out of the oven came my beautiful cakes. Eager to complete the sumptuous layered dessert, I began to frost and stack the round layers as soon as they cooled. What I didn't realize was that I needed to shave the mounded center of each layer before stacking them. (Could it be that I also failed to read the recipe's directions?)

My work was almost complete when the top two layers, balanced carefully over the mound beneath them, split in half! Crumb-filled frosting and large chunks of cake tumbled down the sides of the cake plate and onto the table. What a mess!

I was distraught, but I had no time to start over. I didn't want to waste the cake, so I disassembled each gooey layer and sliced off the rounded tops. (They were delicious, by the way.) I pieced my catastrophe together with extra loads of frosting, slathered on, layer upon layer. Somehow, all the flaws of my messed-up, broken cake vanished under the grace-filled cover of rich, fudgy frosting.

God's rich, extravagant grace covers all our mess-ups, failures, and flaws, much like the thick, fudgy frosting that so beautifully concealed and healed my messed-up flop of a cake.

When we fail, when we make mistakes, when we crumble under the weight of our sin, our heavenly Father lavishes His thick, indulgent grace upon us. He covers our sins and forgives us through Christ's atonement on the cross.

A botched cake is a minor thing; a botched relationship or situation can be major. Maybe you think your failures, mistakes, and mess-ups are beyond repair, can't be covered up or patched back together. Do you wonder how God can forgive the crumbling mess you made? Remember this: no sin, no mess is too much for our Lord to clean up. **Romans 5:8** says, **"But God shows His love for us in that while we were still sinners, Christ died for us."** Did you catch that? *"While we were still sinners."* Recall the similar words we read earlier in **Ephesians 2**, that He made us alive in Christ even while we were dead in our transgressions! He chose you and me and saved us *in the midst* of our sin. He doesn't wait for us to try to get our act together by ourselves (as if we could!). He comes to us in the middle of our mess.

In the Middle of a Mess

Do you want to hear about someone else who made one crumbling mess after another? He was the man we know as the apostle Paul, the writer inspired by the Holy Spirit to pen many of the letters to Early Churches (the Pauline Epistles of the New Testament). The man chosen by God to carry the Good News of Christ to the Gentiles, as well as the Jews. This man, formerly known as Saul, had been a zealous Jew, a Pharisee (religious leader) with great authority. Saul was convinced that he had his act together, but he was sadly mistaken. He was so zealous for the Jewish law, so bent on persecuting followers of the Way (Christianity), that he used his authority to pursue, imprison, and oversee the stoning of early Christians. Years later, looking back, Paul said, regarding his former way of life, **"I persecuted this Way to the death, binding and delivering to prison both men and women" (Acts 22:4)**.

#3 *dig in!*

Read **Acts 26:9–11** to hear more from Paul recalling and lamenting his former way of life. Next, turn to **Acts 7:58–8:1** to see Saul in the middle of his mess, doing the very thing he describes later. Note the connection between the two passages concerning one of Saul's specific actions. How can we tell that he was a man with great authority, and why is that significant here?

Then, right there, in the middle of Saul's mess, Christ came to him. The Lord called him out of the darkness and into the light of His grace! Our Savior chose Saul, speaking to him as he traveled from Jerusalem to Damascus to persecute Christians there too.

#4 *dig in!*

Read this amazing account as recorded in **Acts 9:1–19.** Discuss significant details, especially as they relate to God's lavish grace upon Saul and His work through a disciple named Ananias.

Years later, Paul would share the story of his conversion, how the Lord came to him in the midst of his sin (his mess), showered amazing grace upon him, and chose him for a special purpose. (Check out **Acts 22:4–16; 26:12–18; Galatians 1:13–17**.)

#5 dig in!

Paul spoke plainly and repeatedly of God's grace working in him. Read **1 Corinthians 15:9–10**. How can you tell that Paul, now an apostle chosen by God to spread the Good News, recognized the crumbling mess of his former life? What does Paul say about God's grace here? How can you relate to God's grace in your life?

Chocolate-Frosted Grace, Revisited

As I look back to my chocolate cake catastrophe, I realize that although I was able to cover and "fix" my broken chocolate mess, none of us can fix our sins and our state of brokenness. Brokenness takes many forms: *selfish desires* and *sinful pride, hurtful words* and *lack of forgiveness, critical spirit* and *crippling insecurity, lustful thoughts,* and *failure to reach out to others* with His love (and this is just a sampling).

✁ TAKE A BITE
What precious things of life do you savor the most? How are they fleeting?

#6 *dig in!*

a. *"I've messed up."* We've all made one crumbling mess after another. Incomparably worse than a broken chocolate cake, our brokenness takes many forms. Look again at the list above. In what other ways may we be broken?

Even after the apostle Paul became a humble servant of the Lord Jesus, he admitted his ongoing struggle with sin. We commiserate with Paul, who laments in **Romans 7:19, "For I do not do the good I want, but the evil I do not want is what I keep on doing."**

Only by the Holy Spirit's leading can we, with repentant hearts, acknowledge and confess our sins before the Lord, laying them at the foot of the cross. God, through the glorious riches of Christ, heals our brokenness. He covers all these messes and more with His perfection. Jesus makes us brand-new and mess-free! Christ's blood, shed for us, covers those sins. Our heavenly Father declares our sins forgiven!

b. In what broken messes are you stuck today? Confess those areas of brokenness in which you struggle. If you feel comfortable doing so, write some of them below and share in your group. If you are studying this alone, consider sharing with a pastor, a trusted friend, or a loved one. As you confess your broken mess aloud or on paper, envision yourself laying each sin at the foot of Christ's cross, knowing God lavishes His rich grace and forgiveness upon you in your Savior, Jesus, who heals your brokenness.

Paul's lament over his struggles with sin continues in Romans 7. But notice his sudden switch: **"Wretched man that I am! Who will deliver me from this body of death? Thanks be to God through Jesus Christ our Lord!" (Romans 7:24–25a).** Without taking a breath, Paul answers his own question with the truth of which he is certain! *"Who will deliver me . . . ? Jesus Christ our Lord!"*

Healed!

More than a thick slathering of frosting that effectively conceals the mess we have made, His blood makes us whole where we were once broken; we are healed. The prophet Isaiah foretold, **"But He was wounded for our transgressions; He was crushed for our iniquities; upon Him was the chastisement that brought us peace, and with His stripes we are healed" (Isaiah 53:5).**

#7 dig in!

a. Read the Spirit-inspired words of the apostle Peter in **1 Peter 2:24** as he proclaims the fulfillment of Isaiah's prophecy (above). Write the verse here.

b. What does Peter mean, "that we might die to sin and live to righteousness"?

Looking back to my chocolate cake catastrophe, if I had had time to start over, I might have thrown out the messed-up cake. In our world, we often dispose of messed-up things, don't we? God's Word reveals to us that He thinks and behaves differently. He finds us to be worth salvaging, fixing, healing in Christ. Because of that, you can lay each broken mess at the foot of the cross, knowing that God lavishes His rich grace upon you in Christ to heal your brokenness. That is grace. The grace we *savor*.

Living a Chocolate Life,
we savor God's sweet grace!

PRAYER

Sweet Supplication

Dear Lord, I praise You for Your endless supply of mercy and grace that You have lavished on me, forgiving my sins in Christ and healing my broken mess! Strengthen me by Your Spirit. Lead me to savor this grace that knows no end. In Your name. Amen.

Extravagant Chocolate Three-Layer Cake

3 c. flour

3 c. sugar

1½ tsp. soda

1½ tsp. salt

¾ tsp. baking powder

1 c. + 2 tbsp. water

1 c. + 2 tbsp. buttermilk

¾ c. butter, softened

1½ tsp. vanilla extract

3 eggs

6 oz. unsweetened chocolate, melted

Preheat oven to 350 degrees. Grease and flour three 8- or 9-inch round cake pans. Sift together dry ingredients. Mix sifted ingredients with all remaining ingredients in large mixing bowl. Mix 30 seconds on low speed, then 3 minutes on high. (Batter will be creamy.) Pour batter into prepared pans. Bake 25 to 30 minutes. Cool 10 minutes, then remove layers from pans and cool completely on wire racks before filling and frosting with *Rich Chocolate Frosting*.

Rich Chocolate Frosting:

1 pkg. (8 oz.) cream cheese, softened   ¼ c. butter, softened

2 oz. unsweetened chocolate, melted   Milk

16 oz. (½ bag) powdered sugar (or more)

Cream cream cheese and butter together. Add chocolate and mix well. Add powdered sugar; beat until light and creamy. Alternately add more powdered sugar and a few drops of milk to reach desired consistency and quantity. Frost on completely cooled cake layers, **shaving the mounded center of each baked layer before frosting and stacking!**

*C*hocolate-Savoring Taste Test!

Savor an assortment of chocolate varieties to kick off your Bible study. (What a great way to further a discussion centered on *savoring* God's grace!) Purchase fine chocolate bars: white (at least 20 percent cocoa butter), milk (30–40 percent cacao), semisweet (35–45 percent cacao), bittersweet/dark (50–70 percent cacao), extra dark (70–99 percent), and so forth. You may wish to include special varieties that contain added flavors, fruits, or nuts. Break each bar into small pieces and pass them around, one flavor at a time. Begin by passing around the mildest, lightest colors and flavors, then move on to progressively darker, richer varieties. Pause after each sample to share comments before moving on to the next.

Remember how you imagined savoring an exquisite, rare chocolate? Now, take each real bite-size piece and savor it. For fun, follow the same savoring instructions given when you imagined. Describe the flavors and textures you experience. Can you pick out added flavors? Is it particularly sweet and light or bitter and intense? Is the texture smooth or gritty? (Texture and flavor work together in the chocolate-savoring experience.) After several seconds, you'll notice how the savored delicacy melts, trickles down your throat, and disappears.

Share

A CHOCOLATE SAMPLER

Check all that apply to you, and then discuss as a group:

☑ *You live a chocolate life as you savor God's sweet grace in Christ!
(Share a nugget from the last session and have a Memory Morsel
moment.)*

☑ *You have dipped treats into the liquid treasure of a flowing
chocolate fountain.*

☑ *You have been drawn to chocolate by its rich aroma alone.*

☑ *You think that your favorite chocolate desserts and confections
are simply beautiful!*

☑ *You willingly share your chocolate with loved ones—
most of the time.*

MEMORY MORSEL

*"Therefore be imitators of God, as beloved children.
And walk in love, as Christ loved us and gave Himself up for
us, a fragrant offering and sacrifice to God." Ephesians 5:1–2*

Overflowing Grace

Have you ever observed a chocolate fountain flowing? Thick, gooey liquid
bubbles up and overflows, trickles down, layer upon layer, and spills pools of
chocolate into the basin below.

Have you wondered what it would be like to stand beneath the fountain, allowing the chocolaty liquid to cover you, opening your mouth to catch it and drink to your heart's content?

As we imagine chocolate raining down on us, we can be reminded in another way of the undeserved, freely flowing grace that God pours over us through Christ, even in the midst of our sin. **"The grace of our Lord overflowed for me with the faith and love that are in Christ Jesus" (1 Timothy 1:14).** God's abundant grace and forgiveness lavished on us overflows, spilling onto others so they, too, are able to *smell* and *see* and *taste* God's grace through us. Because we are *living a chocolate life,* by the power of the Holy Spirit, we *share* God's sweet, extravagant grace with others. And sharing grace isn't like sharing chocolate. As we let it flow toward others, it is never depleted! God's favor continuously flows richly over us too.

So how do we flow in grace toward others? **Colossians 3:13** gives us some clear direction: **"Bearing with one another and, if one has a complaint against another, forgiving each other; as the Lord has forgiven you, so you also must forgive."**

#1 *dig in!*

a. Read these powerful words from **Ephesians 4:32–5:2**, which provide direction. God's forgiving love in action for us permeates this passage, which includes this session's *Memory Morsel.* And woven through it are several calls to action for us. What are they? As you find each one, personalize it as you picture someone you may be struggling to forgive.

b. As God's own beloved children in Christ, we are to imitate Him! (And what child hasn't imitated his or her loving parent?) Look at the context surrounding this phrase. The word "therefore" gives us a hint that we should take a look at the words just preceding it (to see what it's *there for!*), as well as the words that follow. What does it look like to imitate God and "walk in love"?

On our own, pouring out God's grace onto others would be impossible. But because His forgiving power is at work in us through the Word, grace can overflow onto those who betrayed us, mistreated us, or hurt us, even onto those who don't seek or deserve our forgiveness. People get to experience the delicious taste of the grace of God in Christ through us as we walk in His sacrificial love. Let's take one more peek at our previous passage:

#2 *dig in!*

"A fragrant offering and sacrifice to God." This beautiful description of Christ in **Ephesians 5:2** is rich in meaning with the history of God's people. Under Old Testament law, priests offered repeated sacrifices to God on behalf of the people; the blood of animals was shed to cover the people's sins. (For further information, take a look at **Leviticus 1.**) As the sacrifices burned on the altar, the smoke of the offerings rose toward heaven, **"with a pleasing aroma to the Lord" (Leviticus 1:9, 13, 17).** Why would the smell of burnt offerings provide an aroma that was pleasing to the Lord?

When Christ, the sinless Son of God, offered His life as payment for the penalty of death for our sins, it was the final and complete sacrifice offered to the Lord, a perfect fulfillment of the Old Testament laws that completely covered the sins of all people for all time. This was a fragrant offering, a sweet sacrifice, perfectly pleasing to God. (Check out **Hebrews 10:1–18**.) In Christ's single sacrifice, we receive forgiveness and salvation! And by His grace-filled work in us, we are able to present our bodies **"as a living sacrifice, holy and acceptable to God"** (see **Romans 12:1**), dedicating our lives to Him, walking in His love, forgiving as He forgave us.

Because of the Spirit's power at work within us, we are able to be kind and tenderhearted, sharing God's *freely flowing favor* with everyone around us. And as we've begun to talk about fragrant offerings and pleasing aromas, let's inhale deeply and read on!

The Aroma of Christ

As chocolate bakes, the fragrance that wafts through the air draws us from across the room to the front of the oven where we pace, impatiently waiting to sink our teeth into the delicacy baking inside. The mouthwatering pleasure we receive from its mere scent elicits a response in us, doesn't it?

As people cross our paths, does the fragrance of Christ waft to them? Are we aromatic reminders of God's love for them? Yes! By the power of the Holy Spirit at work in us, we can spread the Good News of His saving love everywhere, once again *sharing* His sweet grace.

When we share God's freely flowing favor, we spread its sweet aroma and rich flavor as we pass through and touch others' lives. **"Thanks be to God, who . . . through us spreads the fragrance of the knowledge of Him everywhere. For we are the aroma of Christ to God"** (2 Corinthians 2:14–15).

✂ TAKE A BITE:
Who has impacted your life
with his or her sweet fragrance?

Whose lives can you touch
with the aroma of Christ
today? in the weeks ahead?

Picture this: You're in a fine restaurant, and a decadent dessert is carried right past you to the table nearby. As the server delivers a molten lava fudge cake to the delighted diner, the warm scent wafts toward you and you inhale deeply, nearly jumping from your seat to capture the attention of the server before he walks away. "Excuse me! Sir?" You gesture to the woman with the dessert and declare, "I'll have what she's having!"

Ladies, we are the aroma of Christ to God! By the Holy Spirit, His fragrance fills us and permeates us. As Christians, we are called to share the fragrance of the knowledge of Christ with everyone around us. His scent in us elicits a response, and through us, others are drawn to Him. When they catch the fragrance as we share His Word, they will breathe in deeply and exclaim, "Mmmm . . . I'll have what she's having!"

#3 dig in!

a. Open your Bible and take a longer look at **2 Corinthians 2:14–15.** What is the triumphal procession in which Christ is leading us?

b. Again we see the word "fragrance" connected to Christ. Based on what we've already learned from Scripture, share what it means to spread **"the fragrance of the knowledge of Him" (v. 14)** and how that's connected to us being called **"the aroma of Christ" (v. 15)**.

#4 dig in!

God works through us to spread the sweet fragrance of the knowledge of Christ everywhere. As we tell others about our Savior, a perfect place to start is with His saving *grace*. We've been savoring His grace since our first session. What do the following verses confirm and clarify concerning this grace? Think about and discuss opportunities you may have to share these truths in the days ahead.

- Acts 15:11

- Romans 3:23–24

- Romans 5:1–2

- Titus 3:4–7

We pray that every opportunity we take to share His grace and every gift we offer to help another person will rise toward heaven as **"a fragrant offering, a sacrifice acceptable and pleasing to God" (Philippians 4:18)**.

True Beauty

The aroma of chocolate entices us, and the mere sight of it causes our salivary glands to activate! Chocolate is just downright beautiful, isn't it? Visualize with me: cupcakes delicately decorated with sprinkles, golden cookies with dark chocolate chunks, and richly layered chocolate-raspberry tortes. Can we picture anything more attractive? Our hearts palpitate; our heads swim. It's love at first sight!

What really attracts us to these beautiful creations? Is it their outward appearance? Perhaps, but these delicacies could be cleverly created imitations, like a sample dessert display that tempts us to try the edible version. Could the attraction lie instead in our anticipation of the taste—the inner qualities of each treat? We know from experience that when the delicacy is in our mouth, it has truly appealing inner beauty. I believe this is what draws us to chocolate.

What attracts others to *us?* And what does this say of our beauty? We are often trapped into thinking that we will be more compelling to others if we lose weight, have the perfect hairstyle, and wear the cutest clothing, the right makeup, and the most fashionable jewelry. Our society prizes outward beauty, which is vain and fleeting. Our true and lasting beauty, our identity and value as redeemed Christian women, is defined not by outward appearance, but by whose we are in Christ, by the inner beauty we have in Him. We are made in His image (**Genesis 1:26–27**), that we may reflect His character. We are God's beloved (**John 15:9**). We are His children (**1 John 3:1**) and new creations in Christ (**2 Corinthians 5:17**)!

God continues to lavish His grace in Christ upon us, forgiving us for our mixed-up priorities and the world's trappings that often ensnare us. The Holy Spirit fills us with His love and compassion for others, which we *share* in our reverent fear of the Lord. **"Charm is deceitful, and beauty is vain, but a woman who fears the LORD is to be praised" (Proverbs 31:30).** In His strength, we let love flow freely onto an ugly, sin-filled world that watches our every move, looking for *true beauty.*

What is true beauty? When we extend our hands in the name of Christ to carry someone's burden, when we move our feet to walk beside those who would otherwise walk alone, when we offer our ears to listen and our mouths to give words of comfort and cheer, when we share what we have with others (yes, even chocolate!), when we devote our time and our lives for the good of someone else, sharing our hope in Christ as we do, it's beautiful! Attractive! Compelling!

#5 dig in!

Earlier, we read from **Colossians 3:13** for some clear direction about flowing in grace toward others. Open your Bible to this verse, now looking at the immediate context surrounding it. Read **verses 12–14** and envision a picture of true beauty as you "put on" each item listed. On a card, write out this beauty list and encircle the list of words with a heart for a special visual reminder of **verse 14**. Post your beauty list on a mirror.

#6 dig in!

Find further direction about grace in **Romans 12:9–21**. Write down, share, and discuss the true beauty illustrations in this passage that stand out to you as you consider how you may share God's grace with someone He has placed in your path.

The unbelieving world around us is drawn to this inner beauty, and God does something amazing with it. He enables people to see Jesus in us and they are drawn to Him. All we do can cause others to look right through us to the beautiful face of Jesus as He works in and through us. Our imperfect offerings are made perfect in Christ. This is *true beauty*.

Secret Ingredient

While the aroma and beauty of chocolate draw us near and entice us, it's the very taste of our favorite confections that causes our heart to race and our appetite to go into overdrive.

When a friend asked me to share my chocolate chip cookie recipe, I gladly obliged. (I share it with you at the end of this session too.) After attempting my recipe several times, she admitted that she was disappointed. Her cookies never turned out like mine. Hers lacked *taste* and flavor. After more discussion, I found out she was purposely omitting the salt, thinking it unnecessary and unnoticeable. Salt in sweets? Who needs it?! But salt is like a secret ingredient. Leaving out one little spoonful left her cookies lacking.

Salt is my favorite secret ingredient. Just a pinch enhances flavor in almost any dish or dessert. Just a teaspoon makes an entire batch of cookie dough sing with sweet flavor.

#7 dig in!

a. Read **Colossians 4:5–6** and write the verses here. What does the apostle Paul mean when he encourages believers to let their speech be "seasoned with salt"? Earlier, he said to get rid of slander and obscene talk. (See **Colossians 3:8.**)

b. This secret ingredient should permeate all our conversations. **Colossians 4:5** makes specific mention of "outsiders." Why might it be especially important that they hear tasty, salt-seasoned words from us?

No matter how unsalty your speech has been, God forgives you in Christ and gives you the faith and the flavor to begin anew, seasoned with salt, prepared to know **"how you ought to answer each person" (Colossians 4:6)**. Make the most of the time you have.

In the strength of the Spirit, you can *share* the Gospel of grace today, remembering that you are the *aroma* of Christ to God. Through you, others will see the *true beauty* of Christ. And don't forget about *taste*. (Remember to include your secret ingredient!)

Living a Chocolate Life, we share His rich, sweet grace with others!

PRAYER

Sweet Supplication

Lord Jesus, as Your grace overflows for me, enable me to let it flow to others, that I would share this undeserved forgiveness and favor with the world around me, spreading the fragrance of the knowledge of Christ to a world in need of a Savior. Thank You for the inner beauty You give me through faith. Forgive me for any unsavory speech that has come from my mouth. Continually fill me with Your Spirit that my words may be gracious and salty, and that others would be drawn to You through my words and my actions. In Your name I pray. Amen.

Best-Ever Chocolate Chip Cookies

1 c. real butter, softened (not melted)

1 c. brown sugar

1 tsp. vanilla extract

1 tsp. baking powder

2 c. (12-oz. bag) chocolate chips

2 (1.55-oz.) milk chocolate bars, grated

1 c. chopped pecans, optional

2½ c. oatmeal, measured first, then
powdered in blender or food processor

1 c. sugar

2 eggs

2 c. flour

1 tsp. salt

1 tsp. baking soda

Preheat oven to 375 degrees. Cream butter and sugars in mixing bowl. Add eggs and vanilla; continue to beat until light. Add flour, powdered oatmeal, baking soda, baking powder, and salt. Mix well. Fold in by hand the grated chocolate, chocolate chips, and pecans. Chill at least 1 hour or overnight. Spoon dough into 2-inch balls for large cookies. Bake 8 to 10 minutes or until edges are lightly browned and center is moist and chewy. Serve warm with a glass of cold milk, if desired. **Mmm . . . make, bake, and take! Make the most of every opportunity to share these with others as you share His grace!**

Chocolate Chip Cookie Bouquets

Share God's grace *and* this delicious gift! Prayerfully consider who might be the recipient(s) of a cookie bouquet, lovingly baked and crafted. Work individually or as a group. Supplies are few and construction is simple. The appearance, aroma, and taste of this bouquet make it the perfect gift to share!

Directions: Prepare dough for *Best-Ever Chocolate Chip Cookies* (above). Drop **cookie dough** onto pan in uniform sizes using medium or large cookie scoop. Select **long lollipop sticks** (available where cake-decorating supplies are sold) or **wooden skewers** (available in kitchen section of many stores). Insert stick in bottom of each cookie; bake according to recipe directions. (Sticks will be secured as cookies bake and cool.) Cut squares of **cellophane** and wrap cookies individually, then tie **ribbon** around sticks. Place **tissue paper** in bottom and up sides of **clay pot or small basket**. Fit block of **plastic foam** snugly into container. Arrange six to twelve cookie stems in foam and cover foam with more **tissue or paper raffia**. (Add splashes of color to bouquet when choosing ribbon, tissue, and container.) Add a stick with a **Scripture verse** attached and a personal note, as desired. *Suggestion:* **"Oh, taste and see that the Lord is good!" (Psalm 34:8).**

✂ TAKE A BITE

Name some specific examples of *true beauty* in your life. How have you used your hands, your feet, your ears, and your mouth? In what ways have you devoted your time and life for the good of others?

✂ TAKE ANOTHER BITE

Have you listened to your conversations lately? Are they seasoned with salt or lacking in flavor? Do your words build up or destroy?

Satisfaction

A CHOCOLATE SAMPLER

Check all that apply to you, and then discuss as a group:

☑ *You live a rich, chocolaty life as you share God's sweet grace with others! (Share insights gained from the last session, and enjoy a Memory Morsel moment too!)*

☑ *Chocolate-dipped fruits, fresh or dried, are among your chocolate passions.*

☑ *You have driven across town or farther to satisfy a chocolate craving.*

☑ *You feel better after consuming chocolate, your comfort food of choice.*

☑ *You include chocolate on your list of daily needs.*

MEMORY MORSEL

"And my God will supply every need of yours according to His riches in glory in Christ Jesus." Philippians 4:19

Cravings

I'm having a craving, and I want something that will satisfy me! At least one candy bar makes the claim that it *really satisfies*. So this is my theory: if *one* candy bar satisfies, then an entire box of bars ought to make my whole day, right? (Or so my craving says.) *What do you crave?* Chocolate-dipped strawberries? Fresh-baked chocolate chip cookies with a tall glass of milk?

CHOCOLATE FUN FACT
Statistics consistently tell us that chocolate is the food most commonly craved by women in the United States. (Do we really need research to tell us this?)

Grandma's gooey Upside-Down Fudge-Sauce Dessert? (You're in luck! This mouthwatering recipe is just a few pages away.) Or maybe you crave a nice, juicy steak with all the fixings. (Occasionally, cravings do exist beyond chocolate, you know.)

It's quite natural for us to crave our favorite foods. God created us with physical hunger that needs sustenance and craves satisfaction. Our stomach longs to be filled with what satisfies us most. God provided every nutrient necessary to satisfy our physical needs, but He didn't stop there. He created fabulous flavors and vast varieties of foods for us to *enjoy*.

But what about other cravings besides our physical hunger pangs? What do we crave most in life? When do we confuse physical hunger with emotional and spiritual hunger? Maybe we are hungry for *love* because we are lonely. Perhaps we crave *peace* because our world is full of strife. Or maybe we crave *comfort* because we are anxious or afraid, dissatisfied or depressed. God created us with a spiritual hunger that needs sustenance and craves satisfaction.

TAKE A BITE
What foods do you crave the most? Share!

Comfort Food

Give me comfort! Give me love! Give me chocolate! Sound familiar? Have you uttered words like these? Why is chocolate included in many lists of needs? Perhaps because some even call chocolate the ultimate *comfort food.*

We find such pleasure, calming comfort, and soothing satisfaction as we swallow boatloads of our favorite chocolate concoction. Oh, chocolate makes us feel so *good* when we are hurting and hungry! Subconsciously, we're drawn to it because we know it has made us feel better in the past. Research shows that a real physiological response occurs when we eat chocolate. Tryptophan, an essential amino acid found in chocolate, releases the feel-good brain chemical serotonin, which contributes to a temporary boost in our emotions when we indulge in chocolate delights. The resulting euphoric emotions have been compared to the feeling of falling in love.

We know, of course, that the feel-good response is short-lived. Where do we turn for comfort after the last square is swallowed? Is this really a healthy way to seek comfort for what hurts us, to find relief when we are afflicted, to fill a hungry hole that's not in our stomachs but in our souls? I'm all for a little feel-good chocolate, but when does my desire for chocolate become an unhealthy substitute for real pain relief—or my only coping mechanism when I'm feeling blue?

Fillers

In the food industry, fillers are foods that provide little to no nutrition. Also known as *empty calories,* fillers temporarily make a person feel full. They do little to satisfy real hunger; in fact, they leave the body longing for more. Much to my despair, experts have included some near-perfect foods on their *filler* list, foods such as cake, cookies, and chocolate bars. Bummer! I guess that means I need to choose my favorite filler foods sparingly—but my stomach is empty. It growls, and I think it is saying, "Quick! Fill me with chocolate!"

"Wait!" I tell my stomach. "I need to fill you with a good meal first; then we can talk chocolate."

We don't want to deprive our bodies of daily food for our physical nourishment, but what about our souls? There, we find a much deeper hole, a greater emptiness. We may attempt to fill that hole with all kinds of stuff that promises satisfaction. But instead of choosing nutritious, solid food, we often settle for fillers in an attempt to fill our emptiness.

"I'm so lonely! I will feel so much better after I polish off that quart of triple-fudge ice cream." "Maybe someone will finally notice me if I buy that new outfit." "I need those after-dinner drinks to take the edge off my anger." "When I finish this self-help book, I'll finally be happy." "This feel-good movie will make the hurt go away."

We recognize the common cry in these women's words, a cry of hunger and emptiness that longs to be satisfied and filled with love, peace, comfort, and more. While triple-fudge ice cream provides temporary relief, it cannot fill the hurting hole in a heart. New clothes, feel-good movies, and other fillers can't either.

#1 dig in!

a. Your favorite fillers may not be bad, in and of themselves. So why can't any of these things fully and permanently satiate our emotional and spiritual hunger? What's the result when they are used to attempt to fill a hunger for love, peace, comfort, and more?

b. Open your Bible to **Isaiah 55:2**. Isaiah asks a couple of curious questions. On the surface, it appears that he is speaking of physical food. Is he really? What do you think he means when he asks why people are spending their money and labor on that which does not satisfy? How does this also speak to us? What kind of rich food is he referring to, and what does it do for us?

TAKE A BITE
What things do you crave most in life? Maybe you have already thought of more cravings; write them here. We'll discuss our cravings further when we *Dig In*.

God alone provides the perfect, nutritious, soul-satisfying food to fill the hurting hole in us, giving us real sustenance and strength. Only He can fully satisfy. Jesus said, **"Blessed are those who hunger and thirst for righteousness, for they shall be satisfied" (Matthew 5:6).** Jesus offers "food" that revives hungry sinners like you and me: the forgiveness of sin paid for with His death on the cross, new life He gives through His resurrection from the dead, and righteousness that's ours by faith in Him. Only Jesus satisfies our hunger for a Savior!

Satisfied!

In the Gospel narrative recorded for us in John 4, Jesus and His disciples were traveling north from Judea to Galilee. Many Jews would have gone out of their way to avoid Samaria, the land that lay between them and their destination, as they despised the Samaritans. But on that day, there was a special purpose for Jesus' stop by a well just outside a Samaritan town.

#2 *dig in!*

a. Read **John 4:3–15**. What was the reason for Jesus' request for water from the Samaritan woman? What kind of water was He offering *her*, and why would a person never thirst again if he or she drank it?

✄ TAKE ANOTHER BITE
What "fillers" do you choose in order to find something that satisfies? Take a quiet moment to think about and write down the fillers that you choose, or those you've chosen in the past.

b. Now take a look at **verses 16–18**. Jesus made another request of the Samaritan woman. What did He reveal that He knew about her, and why would He ask if He already knew the answer? How might her lifestyle tell us something about her attempts to satisfy her hunger in life? In **verses 25–26**, what did Jesus reveal about Himself?

Jesus brought living water—the gift of eternal life—to a woman who was parched and empty, who was in desperate need of a Savior. He came to her in the midst of her sin and pain, and by His amazing grace, He satisfied her greatest need—her thirst for salvation.

c. Look closely at **verses 28–29** and **39**. Immediately after Jesus revealed to her that He is the Christ, what did the woman do (**vv. 28–29**)? What is surprising about the people's response, considering the reputation she likely had with them (**v. 39**)? What does this say about God's grace, freely flowing through forgiven sinners like you and me?

As Jesus came to this woman, satisfying her *greatest* need, so He comes to each of us, satisfying and supplying our *every* need. **"And my God will supply every need of yours according to His riches in glory in Christ Jesus" (Philippians 4:19).** (That's today's *Memory Morsel!*) In Christ, we are fully and richly satisfied!

Comfort Food for the Soul

Yes, our Savior satisfies our every need. In His mighty power, He fills us with longings for food, as **Isaiah** said (**55:2**), that really satisfies. We yearn for a bountiful supply of *comfort food for the soul*.

We crave a steady diet of *prayer*. We desire heaping helpings of *worship*, where we are fed with the Word and the Sacraments. We hunger for healthy doses of *God's nutritious, delicious Word*, savored, chewed slowly, and digested daily.

1 Peter 2:2–3 speaks of craving God's Word the way an infant craves milk. Just as a baby is satisfied by milk, so those who have **"tasted that the Lord is good" (v. 3)** find that His Word satisfies our deepest needs!

#3 *dig in!*

a. **"For He satisfies the longing soul, and the hungry soul He fills with good things" (Psalm 107:9).** Listen as God's Word in the Psalms speaks to us about the satisfaction only He can give. With what does He provide and satisfy us? As you write down or share, personalize His provision to include your specific needs today. Discuss.

• Psalm 63:1–5

• Psalm 90:14

• Psalm 103:1–5

• Psalm 145:15–16

b. And what is the psalmist's response (and therefore ours!) to His rich provision? Personalize your responses in a prayer of praise to the Lord, who truly satisfies.

God speaks to us across His Word about the things we crave most in life—things like *love, peace,* and *comfort,* as mentioned earlier.

#4 dig in!

LOVE: About our hunger for love, His Word says, **"See what kind of love the Father has given to us, that we should be called children of God; and so we are" (1 John 3:1).** The following verses are just a sampling of God's words of unconditional love to us. Look for specifics that define the depth of His love, and personalize them as you write and share. ("God loves *me* with an everlasting love. . . .")

• Jeremiah 31:3

• Romans 8:38–39

• Ephesians 3:16–19

• 1 John 4:9–10

#5 dig in!

PEACE: We long for peace, and Jesus says, **"Peace I leave with you; My peace I give to you. Not as the world gives do I give to you. Let not your hearts be troubled, neither let them be afraid"** (John 14:27). Read the following verses. What is peace and how do we receive peace with God? Can we have peace in the midst of trials and difficulties? Explain.

• Romans 5:1

• Philippians 4:6–7

#6 dig in!

COMFORT: We hunger for comfort and learn we have a Father **"who comforts us in all our affliction"** (2 Corinthians 1:4). Read the following verses from God's Word, the ultimate comfort food we can savor daily! Recall a time when you received comfort in your suffering or struggles. Were you later able to comfort others in theirs? How can you comfort someone now in a situation similar to yours?

• 2 Corinthians 1:3–4

• 2 Thessalonians 2:16–17

#7 dig in!

God's Word speaks directly to us concerning our every hunger and craving. Our Savior fills us and satisfies every need as only He can. Early in this session when you were asked to **Take a Bite,** did you think of other things that you crave most in life?

How about *security, strength,* and *contentment,* to name a few? Read and personalize a sampling of God's many promises to fill even more cravings:

- *Security:* Psalm 40:2; Proverbs 18:10

- *Strength:* Isaiah 40:29–31; Colossians 1:11–14

- *Contentment:* Philippians 4:11–13; 1 Timothy 6:6–8

- *Others:* Search the Scriptures now or during the week ahead to find for your soul even more food that supplies and satisfies every need.

Women commiserate with one another in our afflictions. Often we bring chocolate to a friend's aid. So go ahead and grab a bit of feel-good chocolate. Take some to a friend who is seeking comfort, looking for something sure to satisfy. But as you do, much more important than a sweet treat is God's Word. Take His *comfort food* with you and share it generously. Share the ultimate comfort we receive, knowing that salvation is won for us in our Savior, Christ Jesus!

Living a Chocolate Life, we find satisfaction in Christ!

Sweet Supplication

Lord Jesus, forgive me for seeking quick fixes to fill my emptiness, my need for You. Thank You for filling me instead with Your faith-giving Spirit. Satisfy my hunger and thirst, my every need, according to Your glorious riches. Lord, You loved me and gave me eternal comfort and good hope through grace. Comfort me, that I may comfort others in Your name. Thank you, Jesus! Amen.

Grandma's Chocolate Upside-Down Fudge-Sauce Dessert

1 c. flour	2 tsp. baking powder
½ tsp. salt	1¼ c. sugar, divided
1 oz. unsweetened chocolate	1 tsp. vanilla
2 tsp. butter	½ c. milk
½ c. chopped nuts	½ c. brown sugar
1 c. cold water	
4 heaping tsp. unsweetened baking cocoa	

Preheat oven to 300 degrees. Grease an 8-inch square baking pan. Sift together flour, salt, baking powder, and ¾ c. sugar. Melt chocolate with butter; blend into sifted ingredients. Blend in milk, nuts, and vanilla; pour batter into prepared pan. Combine cocoa, brown sugar, and ½ c. sugar, and sprinkle over batter in pan. Pour cold water over all. **Important:** Bake at 300 degrees for 40 minutes, then at 350 degrees for 20 minutes. The top becomes crisp, the middle is a warm, moist cake, and the bottom turns into fudgy sauce. This dessert satisfies a chocolate craving like no other when served warm à la mode!

*C*hocolate-Dipped Spoons

Purchase **plastic spoons** (any color), **chocolate melting pieces, clear cellophane**, and **ribbon**. Melt chocolate; dip spoons and lay them on waxed paper until chocolate is firm. Cut cellophane into 8-inch squares and wrap over dipped end of spoons. Tie ribbon to hold cellophane in place. If desired, print labels or small cards with a verse, such as **"He satisfies the longing soul, and the hungry soul He fills with good things" (Psalm 107:9)**; attach verse to spoon handle with ribbon.

The additional beauty of this gift is the reminder of eating that the spoon provides. We hunger for His Word and He satisfies our every need. Choose a time and place to give these small gifts, perhaps along with a *Living a Chocolate Life* devotion book (available at cph.org, item 37-0141). As you give these gifts, share that there is only One who truly satisfies, and allow your gifts to serve as a gracious reminder to every recipient.

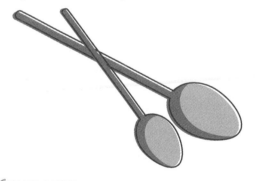

✂ TAKE A BITE
How have these *comfort foods for the soul*—prayer, worship, and Scripture—fed and nourished you? How and where might you dig into them more deeply?

*P*ROMISES

A CHOCOLATE SAMPLER

Check all that apply to you, and then discuss as a group:

- ☑ *You live a chocolate life as you find satisfaction in Christ! (Share a tasty tidbit from the last session that really spoke to you, and enjoy a Memory Morsel moment.)*

- ☑ *You consume dark chocolate regularly for its many promised health benefits.*

- ☑ *You've received a chocolate facial, because chocolate's health benefits aren't limited to consumption.*

- ☑ *You have been rewarded or paid in chocolate.*

- ☑ *You search for healthier versions of chocolate recipes so you can indulge without guilt.*

MEMORY MORSEL

"For all the promises of God find their Yes in Him [Christ]. That is why it is through Him that we utter our Amen to God for His glory." 2 Corinthians 1:20

*B*elieving *P*romises

News Flash! "Dark Chocolate Declared Latest Health Food!" Research reveals evidence that dark chocolate can lower blood pressure and may reduce the risk of diabetes. It contains potent antioxidants too. Forget green tea and citrus fruits; I'm diving into dark chocolate. I'm purchasing eleven pounds

Cacao beans were used as currency by the Mayans, the Aztecs, and in other parts of Latin America for centuries because they were considered so valuable. Can you imagine being paid in chocolate?!

✂ TAKE A BITE

Have you fallen for a deceptive or false promise, temporarily believing it because it sounded so good and you hoped to benefit from it?

of this new health food today. *Eleven pounds?* Yes, that's how much chocolate each American consumes on average in a year, and I'm way behind. I'm hoping to boost that average a bit. (Besides, if dark chocolate is good for me, wouldn't large quantities be *really* good for me?)

Ever notice how quickly we grab onto the latest promise, believing it because it sounds so good? *"Chocolate can be* good *for you"?!* Sure, there is some truth behind this chocolate research, but the promise of better health if we consume as much as possible seems deceptive, doesn't it? Oh, but what a worthy justification for overindulging! I can picture myself now, tossing boxes of chocolate into my shopping cart and justifying my immoderation to everyone near: "I'm investing in my health! The chocolate-covered cherries are mostly fruit! The nut-filled variety? Rich in plant protein! And the chocolate itself? Packed with everything that is heart-healthy!"

As if it weren't enough that chocolate contains so much *promise* as we consume it, we're told that products made with chocolate are also beneficial when applied to our skin. Chocolate scrubs, facial masks, and lotions promise brighter, softer skin, enhanced by chocolate's antioxidants, which protect skin from sun damage, and caffeine, which promotes circulation and helps maintain skin's elasticity. What a promise!

People have been believing *promises* about chocolate for centuries. Two thousand years ago, the Mayans mixed ground cacao beans with bitter spices to make a drink that was believed to be a health elixir. In their culture, the cacao pods were believed to be "the food of the gods." The Aztecs believed the promise that wisdom and power could be attained through consumption of the beloved cacao bean.

The Fine Print

We want to believe promises, especially those that may benefit us. But we don't want to read the fine print on our chocolate label: *"Warning! Contains saturated fat and sugar, known to cause weight gain and high blood pressure. Consume only small portions as part of a healthy diet."* We want to believe so much that we ignore alarms about deceptive or even false promises. We like only the bold print of these claims: *"Look thirty years younger in just five weeks!"* (Thirty years younger than your mother, that is.) *"Drop twenty pounds by eating all the foods you crave!"* (As long as you crave only grapefruit and cabbage.) *"Get guaranteed financial freedom today!"* (Send us all your money, and you won't have any to fret over.)

We may laugh as we read the fine print of these deceptive promises, but there is another, and it's *real.* Also deceptive, and incomparably worse, was this one: **"Did God actually say, 'You shall not eat of any tree in the garden'? . . . You will not surely die. . . .** *[Yes, you will.]* **For God knows that when you eat of it your eyes will be opened, and you will be like God, knowing good and evil"** *[You will fall into sin.]* **(Genesis 3:1, 4–5).** Some promise! Satan lied to Eve in the garden. Eve fell for it. In our resultant sin, we have been falling for his false promises ever since. Satan is the father of all lies, the great deceiver. He wants us to believe these deceptions. He would also have us believe that the promises this world offers us will always deliver. His goal is to take our eyes off the Lord and place our hope and trust in something, *anything* else.

Like every believer before us, as we come to the Lord with repentant hearts in the strength of the Spirit, we are forgiven for all the false promises for which we have fallen. Redeemed and renewed, we rejoice in the One who fulfills His *perfect* promises.

The Great Promise Giver

God is the Father of all truth, the Great Promise Giver. Scripture shows that He faithfully keeps all His promises. We see God's promises fulfilled to His chosen people throughout Scripture. Let's take a look at a sampling:

#1 *dig in!*

As you read the following passages of promise, record each of the Lord's promises that you find, as they are declared or fulfilled.

- Genesis 17:1–8, 15–16; 21:1–2

- Exodus 3:7–8, 16–17

- Joshua 21:43–45

#2 dig in!

God's long-promised provision of a Savior was first announced in the Garden of Eden **(Genesis 3:15),** was foretold for centuries by the prophets, and was perfectly fulfilled in Jesus Christ. Check out these promises in prophecies, which all point to Christ. (These, too, are just a sampling of the many messianic prophecies across the Old Testament.) What details are promised and foretold about the coming Savior? What's so significant about the recurring promise that He will reign with *"justice and righteousness"?*

- Psalm 89:3–4

- Isaiah 9:6–7; 53:3–6, 12

- Jeremiah 33:14–15

In the Book of Acts, the apostles proclaimed the risen Savior, Jesus, in these beautiful words declaring God's greatest promise fulfilled: **"Of this man's [David's] offspring God has brought to Israel a Savior, Jesus, as He promised. . . . And we bring you the good news that what God promised to the fathers, this He has fulfilled to us their children by raising Jesus"** (Acts 13:23, 32–33).

#3 *dig in!*

Read God's words of promise through the apostle Paul in **Romans 4:13–25.** What is the connection between God's promise to Abraham and to us? Who are Abraham's offspring? By faith, what did Abraham believe, and by that same faith, what do we believe? What was "counted to him" that will be "counted to us"?

By faith, we receive God's ultimate promise of eternal life in Christ! **"And this is the promise that He made to us—eternal life" (1 John 2:25).**

Delighted!

As I walked into the church, my eyes feasted upon dozens of tiered cupcake displays decorating an entire room in preparation for a *Living a Chocolate Life* women's retreat. I gazed upon creations with swirled, frosted tops in shades of cotton-candy pink, mint green, and chocolate brown, each complete with sprinkles. I giggled as I wondered if I would get to select from these mouthwatering choices. I was not disappointed! Intrigued by the mint-green frosted variety, I made my selection. The aroma wafted toward me, beckoning me to take my first bite. With paper peeled away, I sank my teeth into the little delicacy, fully expecting the taste and texture to please my palate. I was not disappointed. Much to my surprise, however, in the middle of my bite, hidden smack-dab in the center, was a fudgy, gooey, rich-and-creamy surprise center. Like a kid in a candy shop, this chocolate-loving lady was *delighted!*

We delight in any good thing that brings us pleasure. But nothing this world has to offer—not relationships, work, play, or food—can give us the full and lasting flavor we find when we delight ourselves in the Lord and His promises! **"Delight yourself in the LORD, and He will give you the desires of your heart" (Psalm 37:4).**

✳ TAKE A BITE
In what do you delight your-self? Maybe you take pleasure, as I do, in the sweet surprise filling of a favorite treat. Perhaps you revel in the love of your friends or the antics of your children. You thoroughly enjoy your work. You savor time set aside for your favorite hobby. You relish a gourmet meal or take delight in the decadent dessert that follows.

#4 *dig in!*

Find full and lasting flavor as you sink your teeth into these delights:

- Marvel at His creation every day as you rise. Stand in awe of the One who stretched the heavens and the earth. Pause in delight to read portions or all of **Genesis 1.**

- Praise the One who knit you together in your mother's womb and knows the very number of hairs on your head. Pause in wonder to read **Psalm 139:13** and **Matthew 10:30.**

- Find your greatest joy in Jesus, the one who died and rose for your sins! Rest in Him as you read **John 3:16.**

- Praise the name of the One who clothed you with Christ at your Baptism. Glorify Him as you read **Galatians 3:27.**

Do our mouths water for a heaping helping of His life-sustaining Word every day? Even when we fail to delight ourselves in Him, when we give greater priority to the delights of this world, God's rich mercy in Christ covers us, forgiving our failures and cleansing us from our sins.

The power of the Holy Spirit works in us as we grow in the Word and learn from Him, changing the desires of our hearts to fall in line with His desires. (Read again **Psalm 37:4** above.) He delivers desire to place others' needs ahead of our own and serve them in sacrificial love. He increases our longing to share His saving grace with a world in need of a Savior. He gives us the yearning to grow in His Word. These are even more delightful than the surprise center of a delicately decorated cupcake.

#5 *dig in!*

By faith, we can delight in all the promises God has made to us, as we desire to grow in His Word. As a place to start, look up a few of His many promises in each of these areas. Choose at least one of the following verses to post as a reminder of God's promise to you of His presence; His protection over you; His provision for you; or the purpose for which He has prepared you.

- *Presence:* Deuteronomy 31:8; Psalm 139:1–18

- *Protection:* Psalm 18:2; Psalm 121

- *Provision:* Matthew 6:31–33; James 1:17

- *Purpose:* Ephesians 2:10; Hebrews 13:20–21

#6 *dig in!*

Talk about God's promises as you see them being fulfilled in your life. How have you been reminded of His continual presence? Where have you seen His protection? How has He provided for you? In what ways has He revealed His purpose to you?

God's Promises—Our Delight!

By the Spirit's leading, you can go to God's Word in eager anticipation. Pray that as He reveals truths and promises to you, they may guide you, give you His wisdom, fill you with discernment, and provide you with clear direction. As you read, take it slowly. Savor His words to you. Let them soak in. And dig deeper! Study the context surrounding the verse or passage. Learn the background, the culture, and the history leading up to it, as it applies to each passage.

Remember how dark chocolate holds so much promise? (I've even included a recipe for *Delightfully Dark Chocolate Oatmeal Cake [with Healthier Options]* for your benefit!) While we may delight in its velvety smooth texture, soak up its dark-chocolate flavor, and bask in the health benefits we hope to receive from *a chocolate life*, we delight much more in God's *perfect promises,* proclaimed in His Word and fulfilled in Christ. With joy, we take in every morsel of His truth. It fills and permeates us like nothing else can. **"Your words were found, and I ate them, and Your words became to me a joy and the delight of my heart" (Jeremiah 15:16).**

#7 *dig in!*

a. Find these delicious words of promise, all within **Psalm 119**. Like Jeremiah, devour them! The psalmist asks confidently for each of these things because he is asking them of the Lord, **"according to Your promise" (v. 41)**. The Lord has promised these things for us too! As you read each verse, may it become to you **"a joy and the delight of [your] heart."**

• Psalm 119:41

• Verse 58

• Verse 76

• Verse 116

• Verse 133

• Verse 154

b. Personalize each of the preceding promises to your life and circumstances right now and take each to the Lord in prayer, confident that as you approach His throne of grace (see **Hebrews 4:16**) in the name of Jesus, He promises to answer according to His perfect will.

From the first promise given to the first sinners in the garden, to Abraham who received God's promises by faith, to Moses, to the prophets, and to all of God's people who yearned for the promised Messiah, to every promise recorded across the Scriptures, all of God's perfect promises point to the One in whom they are all fulfilled. Christ. The Messiah. Our Savior. **"For all the promises of God find their Yes in him [Christ]. That is why it is through Him that we utter our Amen to God for His glory"** **(2 Corinthians 1:20).** *(Memory Morsel)*

Living a Chocolate Life, we delight in God's perfect promises, proclaimed in His Word and fulfilled in Christ!

PRAYER

Sweet Supplication

Father God, thank You for the promise of salvation that is mine in Christ! Give me Your strength to trust in all Your promises. Thank You for the many good pleasures in my life, in which I delight. Lead me to take greatest delight in You each day! Make my desires Yours, Lord. In Jesus' name. Amen.

Delightfully Dark Chocolate Oatmeal Cake or Cupcakes (with Healthier Options)

1¼ c. boiling water

1 c. oatmeal

½ c. butter (*Healthier Option:* substitute ½ c. applesauce)

4 oz. dark chocolate (at least 70 percent cacao)

1½ c. flour (*Healthier Option:* substitute whole wheat flour)

1 tsp. baking soda (increase to 1½ tsp. if using whole wheat flour)

1 c. packed brown sugar	1 c. sugar
½ tsp. salt	1 tsp. vanilla

3 eggs

Rich Chocolate Frosting (page 22); *Healthier Option:* powdered sugar

Pour boiling water over oatmeal, butter (or applesauce), and chocolate; stir. Let stand 15 minutes. Preheat oven to 350 degrees. Grease and flour a 9 x 13-inch cake pan. Combine all remaining ingredients except *Frosting* with oatmeal mixture and beat until thoroughly combined. Pour into prepared pan. Bake 35 to 40 minutes. Cool. Frost with *Rich Chocolate Frosting* (or sprinkle with powdered sugar). *Cupcakes:* Scoop batter into paper-lined cupcake pans and bake 18 to 20 minutes. Makes 24.

*C*hocolate Spa Event

Dark chocolate offers health *promises* not only when consumed, but also when applied to the skin, as you learned in today's session. Mix up this recipe for a pampering activity during or following Bible study discussion. (As an alternative, invite others for a chocolate spa event and share a sampling of God's perfect *promises* by reading selections from the *Living a Chocolate Life* devotion book or straight out of this session. Provide samples of your favorite dark chocolate treats too!) Search the Internet for additional chocolate spa recipes and ideas.

REFRESHING CHOCOLATE HAND/BODY SCRUB

1 tbsp. sugar	3 tbsp. unsweetened baking cocoa
1 tsp. pure vanilla extract	3 tbsp. honey
3 tbsp. extra virgin olive oil	

Blend all ingredients to form a paste. Scrub a small amount gently onto your skin. Rinse with warm water. Delight in the aroma as this scrub leaves skin smooth and rejuvenated! Apply rich cocoa-butter moisturizer as desired. Refrigerate remaining scrub in an airtight plastic container.

*F*ROM *S*CRATCH

A CHOCOLATE SAMPLER

Check all that apply to you, and then discuss as a group:

☑ *You live a chocolate-rich life as you delight in God's promises to you. (Share a bite-sized portion from the last session and a Memory Morsel moment too.)*

☑ *You love to bake anything from scratch using real chocolate.*

☑ *You prefer raw cookie dough to baked cookies.*

☑ *You have been fooled by imitation chocolate (but not for long).*

☑ *You watch food channels and search the Internet for chocolate recipes.*

MEMORY MORSEL

"Jesus said to him, 'I am the way, and the truth, and the life. No one comes to the Father except through Me.'" John 14:6

*P*icture *T*his

You are making dessert for special guests. You want it to be the *best*. Memorable. Perfect. One that makes a statement and leaves a lasting impression. It's made with chocolate, of course! This dessert will leave them longing for more, while completely satisfying their chocolate-loving palates. For this special occasion, do you take a shortcut? Do you use a cheap cake mix and serve it with canned frosting? Do you run to the store and grab a cheese-cake from the freezer section? Of course not! You want to give your guests a delectable chocolate delight made from scratch. (Like a made-from-scratch *Chocolate Chip Cheesecake with Chocolate Glaze,* using the recipe at the end of this session.) No shortcuts; only the best will do. After all, your guests are worth the time, effort, and special ingredients that will provide a unique burst of rich, home-baked chocolate flavor and melt-in-your-mouth tex-ture.

Shortcuts

How often are we tempted to take shortcuts in our faith walk and in life? Instead of giving God our very best, we settle. We are too busy to pray. *Wasn't the table prayer enough?* We make excuses for not spending time in God's Word. *Why read the Bible when I'm going to get what I need from the Sunday sermon?* Instead of giving people our very best, we settle. We take shortcuts. *Why go the extra mile for my boss? If I take a few shortcuts on the job, no one will notice. Why read the professor's assignment when there's a summarized version online? If I look like I'm listening to the kids, I can create mental checklists and accomplish twice as much. I said I'd pray for her. Isn't that sufficient? I don't have time to help.* This is just a sampling of our many shortcuts.

Are we giving our best in worship, work, service to our Lord, and care for our family and friends if we take the easy route, the path of least resis-tance, the shortcut?

#1 *dig in!*

a. Take a look at **Mark 12:30–31** and **Colossians 3:23–24** for help in learning what the Lord desires from us concerning these matters. What insights do you receive as you ponder these passages and consider your shortcuts?

b. What do you make of the repetition in **Mark 12:30–31**? Just how much should we give of ourselves as we love? as we work? What do we learn in **Colossians 3:23–24** about service and reward? How could knowing this make all the difference in our work?

Jesus said we should love the Lord with our entire being and love everyone else as we love ourselves. We're to work with all our heart as we remember that we are serving the Lord Christ as we serve others. That's a tall order! Following Jesus' commands leaves no room for shortcuts, does it? And it is possible for us *only* because He first loved us. (Check out **1 John 4:19**.) God demonstrated the extent of His love by sending a Savior to die for our shortcuts, our excuses, our willingness to settle for less than our best. Praise God that He gave His best when He gave us Jesus, when He gave us victory over sin and death, when He gave us new life in Him. His Spirit empowers us and the Gospel frees us to give *our* very best!

Now picture this: You are not making a decadent chocolate dessert this time. You are making time to spend with the Lord, your most special guest, and you want to give Him your very best. As the Holy Spirit works mightily through the Word, He leaves a lasting impression in you. As you savor the Scriptures, you long for more, though you are also fully satisfied. This is *living a chocolate life—from scratch.* It is giving your best to God and everyone He places at your dessert table. You can't wait to invite guests over to share your best with them too!

CHOCOLATE FUN FACT
The phrase "from scratch" is derived from a late-eighteenth-century term for a line scratched in the ground to mark a starting point in sporting events. It came to apply also to the starting point of a competitor who received no handicap, as in "a scratch golfer." From there, it grew to mean "from nothing," and it was increasingly used as a cooking term following the creation of boxed mixes and prepackaged foods. To be made "from scratch" defines a culinary creation as being fully homemade, using only raw ingredients—not a mix.

✖ TAKE A BITE
Where do you take shortcuts?

✖ TAKE ANOTHER BITE
Envision carving out a time and a place each day to meet with your most special Guest! Where might that be? What raw ingredients will you bring with you? A Bible? Maybe a journal? A devotion book? A pen?

No Imitations!

When you are baking from scratch, giving your best, you allow only real ingredients in your recipes, right? Cheap imitation chocolate is *not* allowed! Artificial chocolate-flavored chips are no substitution for real semisweet morsels. There is no substitute for the real thing. One taste, one bite, and your guests would know they had been deceived. Or would they? People would know the difference only if they had tasted real ingredients. If someone had never tried real chocolate, that person could be fooled by a cheap imitation cleverly packaged to look like the real deal.

Just as an imitation morsel looks real enough, so alternate religions outside the Christian faith may have initial appeal. They may look real enough; they may even make alluring claims. Christianity's teachings may sound offensive to ears that want to hear that "all roads lead to heaven," that you can substitute one world religion for another. But the Bible says there are no substitutions. No imitations! Jesus is the *only* way. Only Jesus satisfies our need for a Savior. In **John 14:6, "Jesus said to him, 'I am the way, and the truth, and the life. No one comes to the Father except through Me.'"**

#2 *dig in!*

The apostles—eyewitnesses to Jesus' ministry, death, and resurrection—courageously spread the Good News, and the Early Church exploded in growth. Read **Acts 4:12** and write it here. What does the apostle Peter boldly proclaim, and how does it parallel Christ's words in **John 14:6** above?

While cheap imitation chocolate won't actually hurt someone, dabbling in alternate religions or believing false claims about Christianity will. Our culture wants to mix world religions, adhering to some Christian truths while claiming teachings and beliefs of religions outside the one true faith. But God's Word leaves no room for mixing. Other teachings and religions are *not* alternate roads to heaven, to salvation, to eternity with God. Without Christ, humans face eternal damnation and separation from Him. Many may attempt to deceive us by claiming something about Christ while twisting His words, trying to convince us that we must earn our salvation. Some reject His death and resurrection, even denying that He is God's Son, claiming instead that He was merely a man or a prophet.

As Jesus teaches about the end times, He begins by warning believers not to be deceived. **"See that no one leads you astray. . . . Many false prophets will arise and lead many astray" (Matthew 24:4, 11).**

#3 *dig in!*

Paul gives specific warnings to Christians in **Acts 20:29–30; 2 Corinthians 11:13–15; Galatians 1:6–9;** and **2 Peter 2:1–3.** What will happen or is already happening that Paul warns believers about?

Be a Berean!

We must be cautious of the claims we hear. "Be a Berean!" the apostle Paul would surely tell us if he were here today. As he traveled on his missionary journeys, preaching the Gospel of Jesus Christ to the people, he noticed something special about the Bereans.

#4 dig in!

Read **Acts 17:10–12.** What was it about the Bereans that caught Paul's attention? What did he notice that was noble about them? How can we see by the people's response that Paul's message of proclaiming Christ as the promised Messiah did, in fact, fulfill the Old Testament prophecies?

We would be wise to do today as the Bereans did then. We must test everything we hear today against God's Word, the Scriptures. That means keeping our ears open for *imitation* claims coming across television, over the Internet, via books and music, and even in churches. If we don't know what God's Word says, we may fall for anything.

#5 dig in!

None of us wants to be deceived. To "be a Berean" and test everything against Scripture, we must be students of the Word and learn from it. How do God's Words in **Psalm 119:9–16** and **Colossians 3:16** encourage us to stand strong in the one true faith?

Not only is the Bible the inspired Word of God, but it is also a means by which He gives us His grace. The Holy Spirit works powerfully through the Word, creating and increasing faith, imparting truth, and guiding us into greater understanding. The Bible tells us that only by faith in Christ, God's Son and our Savior, will we be saved. God saved us not by works, but by grace alone through faith alone. This is the truth of the Gospel on which we stand. (See again **Ephesians 2:8–9**.) Praise God for His free gift of faith and salvation in Christ!

#6 *dig in!*

a. God tells us in **1 John 4:1–4** to **"test the spirits,"** to examine words and actions against Scripture. Read this passage; what specific guidance does He give in discerning whether or not a spirit is from God?

b. **Verse 4** gives us beautiful reassurance. Personalize this truth, inserting your name as you read it aloud (even together as a group), since you are His "little children" too. How have we "overcome them," the spirits of the antichrist in the world?

✂ TAKE A BITE

Have you recently detected imitation faith claims because you knew they didn't hold up to God's Word of truth? (For example, pithy statements frequently flash before us on social media, in films, and in print; they mention God's name, but make claims contrary to His Word.) Describe these claims here:

The Real Deal

Remember when we talked about aroma, inner beauty, and taste in Session 2? The sweet, satisfying richness of God's grace in Christ attracts people when they notice Him at work in us. With the help of the Holy Spirit, they see in us the *real deal*. Nothing artificial. No imitations. They see His grace and forgiveness at work. Our salvation does not depend upon our good works, as many followers of other religions believe, so they are shocked that we go out of our way to love them. We love them because Christ's love and His power work in us and enable us to do so. We love them as Jesus loves them. Whether or not they realize it, they desperately need to know the Truth. The Real Deal. Christ.

> *But in your hearts honor Christ the Lord as holy, always being prepared to make a defense to anyone who asks you for a reason for the hope that is in you; yet do it with gentleness and respect. (1 Peter 3:15)*

#7 *dig in!*

a. Chosen in Christ and saved by His grace through faith, we have *The Real Deal*. But many people have never heard of Him; others have heard only confusing imitation claims and have fallen prey to false teachings. As stated in 1 Peter above, they may ask us for a reason for the hope that is in us. How can we be prepared to answer them?

b. What is so significant about the first part of this verse, as it relates to the rest? Why is the last part of this verse also important as it, too, relates to the rest?

God's work in us enables others to see, smell, and taste the difference. What makes Christianity different than all the rest? *Grace* . . . God's sweet, amazing grace in Christ.

Living a Chocolate Life from scratch in the one true faith!

PRAYER

Sweet Supplication

Dear Lord, fill me with the desire to live a chocolate life—from scratch. Empower me by Your Spirit to give my best to You and to everyone You place at my table. Father, forgive me when I have faltered, listening to the imitation claims of others instead of Your truth. Continually fill me with Your Spirit and point me to Your Word, that others may be attracted to Christ through me. In His precious name I pray. Amen.

Chocolate Chip Cheesecake with Chocolate Glaze

Crust and Cheesecake filling:

2 c. chocolate cookie wafer crumbs

¼ c. melted butter

3 (8-oz.) packages cream cheese, softened

½ c. sugar

2 tbsp. flour   1 tsp. vanilla

2 egg whites   1 c. heavy cream

½ c. *real* mini semisweet chocolate chips, or more if desired

Preheat oven to 375 degrees. Starting *from scratch,* mix cookie crumbs and melted butter; press into bottom of 9-inch spring-form pan. In large bowl, combine cream cheese, sugar, flour, and vanilla. Beat with an electric mixer until fluffy. Add egg whites, beating on low speed until combined. Stir in cream and chocolate chips by hand. Pour mixture into crust-lined pan.

Place on baking rack in the middle of the oven, with a shallow pan of water on a lower rack directly below it. (This prevents cracking in cheesecake.) Bake 35 to 40 minutes or until center appears nearly set when shaken. Do not overbake. Cool to room temperature in pan on wire rack. Loosen sides with knife, then gently remove sides of pan.

Let cheesecake cool completely, then top with *Chocolate Glaze.*

Chocolate Glaze:

½ c. *real* mini semisweet chocolate chips

¼ c. heavy cream

Melt chocolate chips with cream in small heavy saucepan; cook and stir until thickened and smooth. Immediately spread over cooled cheesecake. Cover loosely and chill at least 4 hours.

Cookie Mix in a Jar

Create and give away your very own mixes—made *from scratch*—and share with each recipient what it means to *live a chocolate life* from scratch in the one true faith!

Using the *Best-Ever Chocolate Chip Cookie* recipe from Session 2, carefully layer all dry ingredients in a **2-quart wide-mouth glass jar**. (Blend oatmeal and grate chocolate bar first.) Pack each layer as necessary to fit. Add lid and decorate with **ribbon or fabric**, as desired. Attach **tag** with list of remaining ingredients, along with the following instructions: *Empty mix into large mixing bowl. Add 1 c. softened butter, 2 eggs, and 1 tsp. vanilla extract. Mix well by hand. Chill at least 1 hour or overnight. Spoon dough into 2-inch balls for large cookies. Bake at 375 degrees 8 to 10 minutes or until edges are lightly browned and center is moist and chewy.*

*B*ITTERSWEET

A CHOCOLATE SAMPLER

Check all that apply to you, and then discuss as a group:

- ☑ *You live a chocolate life from scratch, in the one true faith! (Share a sample that really spoke to you from the last session, and have a Memory Morsel moment too.)*

- ☑ *You have been tricked into trying bitter baking chocolate (100 percent cacao)!*

- ☑ *You prefer really dark chocolate (70 percent cacao or higher).*

- ☑ *You have made molded chocolates.*

- ☑ *You prefer nut- or cream-filled chocolates to plain.*

MEMORY MORSEL

"And we know that for those who love God all things work together for good, for those who are called according to His purpose." Romans 8:28

*B*itter

My love for chocolate was already strong when I was quite young. And I knew there was a big box of baking bars in my mother's cupboard. Would she even notice if I snuck just one bar from the box? Doubtful. So I climbed the cabinets one day, grabbed the box, and stole a bar. *Mmm!* It sure smelled like the real thing. Ever so sneakily, I popped it into my mouth and began chewing. *Ugh! Yuck! Eww!* I was old enough to know that chocolate was a good thing, but young enough that I didn't understand the meaning of "Unsweetened Baking Chocolate." My naïve expectation of something rich and sweet was dashed by a blast of bitter, unsweetened nastiness—100 percent pure cacao! My happy chocolate-sneaking smile was replaced with an unhappy puckering grimace as I attempted to rinse my mouth out to erase the bitter taste.

Where I had hoped for something sweet, I received something bitter instead. Life is kind of like that sometimes too. Where we hope for sweet morsels of happiness, we sometimes receive bitter nuggets of pain and suffering. In our sin, we allow ourselves to become embittered by the circumstances into which we are often dipped, to be disappointed by the effects of the world that threaten to change our taste and leave a bitter aftertaste.

How can we maintain a sweet outlook on life when there is so much bitterness, so much anger, hurt, and heartache? Bitter feelings are often packaged in unsweetened circumstances. One woman struggles with anger against her malicious co-workers who ridicule her for her faith. Another cannot let go of her hurt to reconcile with her loved ones. Another lives with chronic pain and the fear of news she suspects her doctor has for her. Still another woman aches from the heartache of losing the person she held most dear.

How do we survive these circumstances and so many more like them? What do we do when we're crushed under the weight of sorrow or pain? How can we not become embittered when we're brokenhearted or angry? To what may we resort in our attempt to erase the bitter taste of our troubles?

✂ TAKE A BITE

Into what bitter circumstances or suffering have you been *dipped* lately? Has it left a bitter taste in your mouth?

Many of us turn to something we think will remove the bitter taste: food, sleeping pills, alcohol, fantasy escape, gambling, extramarital affairs, gossip, binge shopping, and more. We find something that we've convinced ourselves will numb the emotional pain, sweeten the flavor of our dark days, or at least offer a distraction from our misery. But that something never delivers real relief from our troubles; it cannot heal our broken heart; and it often causes an even nastier taste. We may have rationalized the distractions we've chosen, and maybe we've tried to find a solution on our own, seeking help through self-talk, to no avail.

Can our sweetness be restored? Is there a real solution, a true answer? Yes. And our Savior, Jesus, has that answer. He says, **"Come to Me, all who labor and are heavy laden, and I will give you rest" (Matthew 11:28).** We can take our pain and sorrow to the One who went to the cross, tasting the bitter pain, suffering, and death that should have been ours. **Hebrews 2:9** reminds us that Christ tasted death for everyone. He knows our anger, hurt, and heartache. Our compassionate Lord feels our pain. His blood covered our sins and the sins of the whole world; sweet salvation is ours in Christ! Jesus rescues and gives *real* rest. When we lean into His strong arms instead of striving to earn grace and attempting to restore sweetness on our own, we receive His forgiveness, healing, and hope.

#1 *dig in!*

Are you brokenhearted? facing troubles? crushed in spirit? Cry out to your Rescuer, who says, "Come to Me." Read **Psalm 34:15–18** and see what happens when you do! How can you respond in faith when it doesn't seem that you're being delivered out of your troubles?

#2 *dig in!*

In the middle of every circumstance, you can turn to the Bible and cling to your Savior's words, trusting that His loving grip is upon you. Turn to His comforting Word now. In these verses, how does God reveal His constant care over you, on the days that are light and smooth and on those that are dark and lumpy, and especially at the center of every trial and difficulty? Write key words as reminders from each verse and post them where you will see them every day.

• Deuteronomy 31:8

• Psalm 73:23

• Isaiah 43:1

• Zephaniah 3:17

Overcome!

We can rest assured even in the middle of our trials that we have a Savior who is bigger than every tribulation we will ever face. As Jesus was comforting His disciples just before His arrest and crucifixion, He told them that *because* they were His followers, they would face persecution, sorrow, and trials. (See **John 15:20**.) But with these words He included a promise: **"In the world you will have tribulation. But take heart; I have overcome the world" (John 16:33).**

#3 *dig in!*

a. Bitter circumstances will be a part of every believer's walk and may sometimes be the direct result, as we are mocked and even persecuted for our faith. As His followers today, we shouldn't be surprised when we suffer because of Christ. What does the Lord say through Peter in **1 Peter 2:19–23** and **4:12–14** about suffering as a Christian?

b. What example did Christ leave us for how to respond when suffering for our faith (**1 Peter 2:23**)? How can we possibly *rejoice* and even be *blessed* when we suffer in this way? (See **1 Peter 4:14**.)

Today, Christ comes to us in His Word and the Sacraments, providing His strength to not only *endure* our trials, struggles, and suffering, but even more, to ultimately *overcome* them victoriously through Him who has overcome the world at the cross and the empty tomb!

Mixed and Moldable

Sometimes all we see of our circumstances is the place of suffering in which we live; we cannot see the future result in the midst of our trials. But God can. From our limited taste, we may know only the bitter moments, and they are nasty by themselves.

Similarly, unsweetened chocolate, sugar, butter, and vanilla—basic candy ingredients—are not delectable delights on their own. In fact, separately, each is hardly palatable. (Have you tried swallowing several cups of sugar? or consuming an entire stick of butter? or sipping straight vanilla? None is a tasty treat by itself.) However, when a chocolatier *mixes* these ingredients together in the correct quantities, at the precise time, and heats them to the perfect temperature, all the unpalatable ingredients work together to form a *chocolate candy sensation.* (A sensational candy recipe awaits you at the end of this session too.)

God allows a variety of circumstances, some bitter and some sweet, to *mix* together in our lives, in His order and according to His timing (big chunks of one thing, little sprinklings of another).

CHOCOLATE FUN FACT

Melting chocolate is a delicate process. If it is overheated or if moisture is accidentally added during the melting process, the chocolate *seizes*. It suddenly becomes stiff, lumpy, thick, and unworkable. Why? Too much heat or water causes the cocoa solids to separate from the cocoa butter and creates a stiff, unyielding paste.

Chocolate is beautifully moldable, able to take on whatever shape a chocolatier chooses. To create his moldable masterpiece, however, the chocolatier must use just the right amount of heat to melt the hard block of chocolate. Too much heat causes chocolate to seize and become even stiffer. Too little heat leaves chocolate too firm and unyielding.

In a similar way, God, our "great chocolatier," has a special shape in mind for each of us. He uses the heat in our lives to soften our hardened, bitter hearts, unyielding pride, and stubborn attitudes. In His perfect wisdom, He allows just the right amount of heat—pain or discomfort—to soften us, to lead us to see our need for our Savior, who died to save us from these stubborn sins and so many more.

As He works in us, making us moldable, we can ask Him to give us eyes to see beyond our circumstances and the similar situations of others. Instead of asking, "Why?" we can pray for discernment by asking, "How will You use this?" We ask for greater trust to believe that He has a purpose beyond our limited view of this distasteful moment. We don't deny our bitter realities and present suffering, but by the Spirit's strength, we can trust that His plans include much more than what meets the eye.

#4 *dig in!*

Go ahead! Ask, *"How will You use this, Lord?"* Approach God's throne of grace with confidence (see **Hebrews 4:16**). While He may not reveal that answer to you now, you can ask for greater trust and obedience to follow His lead, according to His Word. What do the following verses have to say about God's plans and purpose for you? How might they guide you in your prayer now?

• Psalm 57:2

- Proverbs 19:21

- Isaiah 55:8–9

- Jeremiah 29:11

#5 *dig in!*

a. **Romans 5:3–5** and **James 1:2–4** speak to our sufferings and trials, which can test our faith. Both passages begin with a call to respond in what way? Through these verses, we learn that our suffering and trials produce many Christlike qualities in us, as He helps us in our suffering and molds and transforms us through our trials. Make a list of these Christlike qualities. By God's grace, where have you seen some of these being produced and growing in you? As a result of what trials?

b. According to **Romans 5:5,** what is significant about the hope that is produced as a result? In **James 1:3,** what is meant by "steadfastness"? If it "has its full effect" (**v. 4**), does that mean we will achieve perfection this side of heaven?

Through our trials and sufferings, our faith grows stronger. **"And after you have suffered a little while, the God of all grace, who has called you to His eternal glory in Christ, will Himself restore, confirm, strengthen, and establish you" (1 Peter 5:10).** We yield to His touch as He transforms us and then makes us stronger than we were before; we are confirmed and established in Him. Our sweetness is restored!

Under the care of the Great Chocolatier, **"We know that for those who love God all things work together for good, for those who are called according to His purpose" (Romans 8:28).**

#6 *dig in!*

How could you gently share **Romans 8:28** *(this session's Memory Morsel)* in your own words with someone who is seeking guidance and reassurance from the Lord in the middle of a sour circumstance? What might you humbly add from your own past experiences, while also recognizing that no two trials are the same?

#7 *dig in!*

In God's revelation of heaven to John, our Lord gives us a glimpse of eternity before His throne. How can **Revelation 21:3–4** bring you great comfort in the midst of every unsavory circumstance you may face now or in the days to come? (See also **2 Corinthians 4:16–18** for Paul's perspective concerning his present suffering in light of eternity.)

With certainty of eternal life, where we will be gathered around His throne of grace, we are given the strength and joy to live to the fullest through each circumstance, no matter what it contains! We can **"give thanks in all circumstances; for this is the will of God in Christ Jesus for [us]" (1 Thessalonians 5:18).**

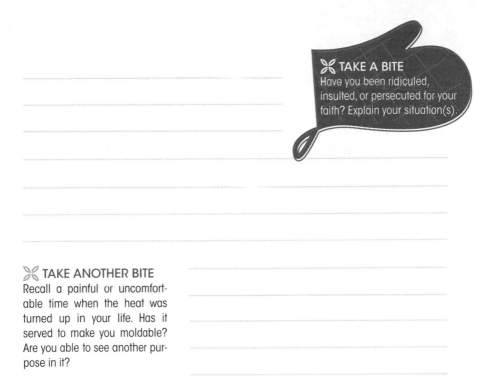

✂ TAKE A BITE
Have you been ridiculed, insulted, or persecuted for your faith? Explain your situation(s).

✂ TAKE ANOTHER BITE
Recall a painful or uncomfortable time when the heat was turned up in your life. Has it served to make you moldable? Are you able to see another purpose in it?

Molded Masterpieces

Although heat and change can be painful and difficult, God is molding and shaping us into the masterpieces He called us to become. We were made in the image of God **(Genesis 1:27).** And our Great Chocolatier, through the work of the Holy Spirit, continues to lovingly mold us into Christ's likeness, by His glory, shaping us and transforming us to become more like Him **(2 Corinthians 3:18).**

The most exquisite molded chocolates are also cleverly and uniquely marked by a specific swirl or stamp on top. Connoisseurs know the inside by the outside. As we are molded into Christ's image, we are recognized by His specific imprint upon us. In our Baptism, each of us was marked by Christ as His own child, unique and recognizable. We are His molded masterpieces. Connoisseurs or not, others recognize those who are molded and marked by Christ. Our words and actions show that the Spirit dwells inside us. And when we melt in failure, He forgives, reshapes, and strengthens us to start anew. Oh, that the world would be drawn to Christ through us the way one is drawn to a particularly fine molded chocolate!

Whatever the flavor of our days, we trust God's care over all the details of our lives, knowing that He can make something sweet out of our bitter circumstances. The sweet love of Christ permeates us and enables us to *live a chocolate life*. The Holy Spirit transforms us and shapes us, making us more like Christ. **"He who began a good work in you will bring it to completion at the day of Jesus Christ" (Philippians 1:6).** Our Redeemer lavishes His rich, sweet grace upon us as He continues His good work in us until the day of His return.

Living a Chocolate Life, we are sweet in bitter circumstances, by the grace of God!

PRAYER

Sweet Supplication

Lord, forgive me for my faulty focus on bitter circumstances instead of on You, who works all things together for good. Help me trust You to make something sweet out of the bitter circumstances in my life. Thank You for sweet salvation in Christ, for choosing me and forgiving me, a hardened and unyielding sinner. Continue to soften me, shape me, and mold me into Your image as Your masterpiece! In Jesus' name. Amen.

Chocolate Candy Sensation: Fudge!

1½ oz. unsweetened chocolate	½ c. milk
⅓ c. light corn syrup	2 c. sugar
2 tbsp. butter	1 tsp. vanilla extract

Mix all ingredients except vanilla in saucepan and bring quickly to a boil. Turn fire very low and boil for exactly 5 minutes. Remove from heat and stir in vanilla. Cool and beat with wooden spoon until right consistency. (The secret to this chocolate candy sensation is allowing it to cool before beating, which will give it a creamy, not grainy, texture.) Drop by teaspoonfuls onto waxed paper; cool completely, and store at room temperature in airtight container.

✂ TAKE A BITE

How are you able to recognize another "molded masterpiece" in the making? What is it about that person that makes him or her unique and recognizable?

Making Molded Chocolates

Enjoy this wonderful opportunity to continue group discussion about becoming moldable and shaped in the Lord's image. You'll find **candy molds** and **melting chocolate** in the candy-making section of many hobby and variety stores.

Directions: Melt chocolate according to package directions until smooth and *moldable.* Spoon chocolate into each mold until level full; lightly tap on counter to eliminate air bubbles in chocolate. Place in refrigerator or freezer until candy is set. Unmold by inverting mold just above waxed-paper-covered surface. Gently tap mold; shaped and molded chocolate masterpieces will appear. (You can create additional shapes, colors, and flavors using a variety of molds, **candy melts**, and **flavoring extract oils**.) Arrange molded chocolates in small containers or gift boxes to display, share, and give away. Create a gift tag with Scripture, or create miniature notes to tuck with each chocolate, using phrases like the following: "You are molded in Christ!" "Filled with the sweet love of Christ!" "You are God's molded masterpiece!" *Additional idea:* Invite a chocolatier to give a candy-making demonstration.

SESSION 7 Gifts

A CHOCOLATE SAMPLER

Check all that apply to you, and then discuss as a group:

☑ *You live a rich, chocolaty life as you become sweet, even in bitter circumstances, by the grace of God. (Share an important insight from the last session and enjoy a Memory Morsel moment.)*

☑ *You love to give chocolate-themed gifts.*

☑ *You've saved your chocolate for so long that it has changed color.*

☑ *You have a special memory of receiving a chocolate gift for your birthday, Valentine's Day, Christmas, or another special occasion.*

☑ *You own a chocolate sign, T-shirt, or bumper sticker.*

MEMORY MORSEL

*"Now there are varieties of gifts, but the same Spirit;
and there are varieties of service, but the same Lord; and
there are varieties of activities, but it is the same God who
empowers them all in everyone." 1 Corinthians 12:4–6*

Saved Gifts

My children, when they were young, loved to receive chocolate candy gifts just as much as the next child. However, they developed a tendency to hoard them. Some kids devour every bit of chocolate in their assortment boxes, baskets, treat bags, or stockings, leaving a large pile of wrappers and an even larger tummy ache as the only evidence. Not my children. They would savor a piece or two, then carefully count and label their stockpile and put it on the shelf. Then they'd forget all about their stash, and I would have to stare at its tempting chocolate goodness. (It was clearly off-limits because it was not labeled with my name!)

Eventually my children would rediscover their months-old chocolate stash, only to find stale, hard, strange-colored chocolate inside. Chocolate has a short shelf life, and their saved gifts often appeared to be spoiled.

How often do we carefully set aside many of God's rich and splendid gifts, saving them for the right opportunity, only to neglect to use them entirely? We set His Word on the shelf. We fail to serve or reach out to others. We neglect to share what we have so generously been given. We don't use His gifts as we ought.

God's greatest gift of faith is freely given and instilled in us by His Holy Spirit in our Baptism and through the Word. It fills us, enabling us to believe in our Savior, Jesus Christ, whose death and resurrection paid for our sins, our neglect of His Word, and our many failures. The Spirit also gives us other gifts and the ability and desire to use them, that we may share His grace with others and begin glorifying Him *now*. Let's begin by growing in His Word . . . *now!*

Growing Up

#1 *dig in!*

a. Read **Ephesians 4:11–16**. What is the role of pastors and shepherds, and what's the purpose of equipping and building? How are all members of the Body involved in the "work of ministry" (**v. 12**)?

b. The last two verses of this passage, **verses 15–16**, talk about growth. How do we "grow up"? Who is the Head of the Body? What happens when each part is working properly?

As members of the Body of Christ, we are united, built up, and strengthened by the Gospel, that we may use the good gifts with which God has richly blessed us. As we do, we participate in the work of ministry, sharing the love of Christ in our vocations.

By the Spirit's leading, may you continue to grow up in Christ. Respond to His loving invitation to grow in the Word, that you may be prepared for Christian service, using His good gifts!

Gifts from God

Everything we possess is a gift from God, given by His grace to be used to benefit others and to glorify Him. Our gifts are the instruments through which we get to share God's sweet grace with other believers and with those who need to hear of His saving love.

CHOCOLATE FUN FACT
Chocolate usually appears shiny, but don't assume it has spoiled if the surface has developed a mild gray or white appearance. This outer change is called "bloom" and it reveals that the chocolate has undergone changes in temperature. The texture and taste are usually only mildly affected.

#2 *dig in!*

Read **1 Peter 4:10–11.** How do the two gifts stated here encompass many of the specific gifts we may possess? What do we learn about the use of each gift?

#3 *dig in!*

God gives us a brief picture of the vast varieties of His gifts in this session's *Memory Morsel,* **1 Corinthians 12:4–6.** Take a closer look and make note of the powerful threefold repetition of two important truths. What's different and what's the same? Personalize these to your role(s) as a member of the Body of Christ.

Vital Ingredients

Our very favorite chocolate recipes contain a wide variety of ingredients. Take, for example, my much-loved *Triple Chocolate Rocky Road Brownie Pizza* (the recipe follows at the end of this session). It cannot fully satisfy my cravings if even one item is left out because each ingredient plays a special role in the making of the whole. At a glance, I know that I will delight in a dessert containing chocolate chips, nuts, and marshmallows and topped with chocolate drizzle. But while these ingredients are the most noticeable, that doesn't make their contribution to the pizza more or less significant than other ingredients. Under the tasty toppings lies the brownie base, which contains several vital ingredients. Without sugar, where would I find sweetness? A spoonful of vanilla and a scoop of cocoa add bursts of flavor. Flour and butter give the pizza a chewy, moist consistency. I don't see the eggs, but if omitted, the batter would not hold together or rise quite the same. Without each and every ingredient, it wouldn't be the brownie pizza it was intended to be.

Have you ever thought of yourself as a vital ingredient? You are! You are an indispensable member of the Body of Christ!

#4 *dig in!*

With the dessert pizza in mind, read **1 Corinthians 12:12–25.** Now study the passage slowly, inserting the reference for the verse(s) to which I'll allude in the following fun examples; and as you do, envision the Body of Christ and each member as a vital part of the one Body.

- If the flour should say that since it's not a chocolate chip, it doesn't belong to the pizza, that wouldn't make it any less a part of the pizza.

- If all were a single ingredient, where would the dessert pizza be?

- As it is, there are many ingredients, yet one pizza!

- All ingredients in the pizza have the same care for one another.

Whatever your role, it is indispensable to the Body as a whole. God gives gifts as He knows best (**v. 18**). They may seem disproportionate to us (sometimes it seems the chocolate chips get all the attention), but only because we cannot see the bigger picture or the finished result in the way that God can. Maybe your gifts are noticed by others, or maybe they blend in with those serving behind the scenes. Maybe your role in the Body of Christ, like the blended ingredients in the pizza's brownie base, is to add sweetness, flavor, or consistency. Every member of the Body, regardless of his or her role, works to *hold together* the whole! God uses every one of His chosen ingredients for His purpose and His glory.

Using God's Good Gifts

"Every good gift and every perfect gift is from above" (James 1:17). When we talk about being faithful stewards (look again at **1 Peter 4:10**) with the good gifts God has given us by His grace, we can refer to His gifts as *treasures, time,* and *talents.* To be a steward is to use God's good and perfect gifts that we've been given, according to His will, sharing them with others.

> **TAKE A BITE**
> Consider some of the personality traits, skills, and talents that you possess. What comes to mind right away? And how are you uniquely packaged within your surroundings, family, and circumstances?

Treasure

Perhaps you have been blessed with material treasures you can share, as an expression of God's love, to assist those in need and to assist with the growth of God's kingdom. Maybe your funds will help a local church or ministry agency, or support a needy child or mission on the other side of the world. Could your treasures contribute to filling a food pantry? Have you been blessed with clothing or furniture that you could give to a neighbor in need or to an organization that reaches out to those who need to start over? God works through our humble offerings to bring the message of salvation next door *and* all over the globe!

#5 *dig in!*

a. Turn to **2 Corinthians 9:7–8**. What does **verse 7** say about the attitude of our hearts as we give of our treasures? How can we become cheerful givers?

b. What's so significant about the repetition of "all" in **verse 8**? How is God at work, and what happens in and through us as a result?

Time

We are all given the gift of time, although many of us wonder what happens to it! It's easy to envision storing up our treasures, but what about time? When we fail to use our time wisely or choose to use it only for selfish purposes, we neglect to use God's gift as He intended. We praise Him for His great gift of grace that continues to pour down over us, even when we've misused any of His good gifts (treasures, time, or talents). And we look to His strength to lead us and enable us to give again.

#6 *dig in!*

In **Ephesians 5:16** and **Colossians 4:5,** we are encouraged to do something that concerns our time. What is it? How can you do this as you consider your relationships, interactions, and opportunities, and as they intertwine with God's desire for you to impact the world for Christ? Discuss.

Use God's precious gift of time in your church and community, in your home and school. Learn where service is needed in local ministries or in stateside or overseas mission work. By His grace, you can *make the best use of your time* for the good of others and the advancement of the Gospel. As you give the gift of time, God will use you to have an immediate and eternal impact on others' lives.

Talents

God has given each of us talents, abilities, and personalities that are unique to us. Picture an enormous box of assorted chocolates. Each candy is filled with something delicious and different. Similarly, God fills us with personality traits and skills that He creatively chose for His special purpose. Maybe we haven't even discovered all of them yet. Adventures await as we uncover and explore our God-given talents and gifts!

You have a one-of-a-kind shape and flavor, created from a set of ingredients God used just for you. And your life is packaged like no other.

Romans 12 gives us a list of gifts that we may draw from, and once again, we see the word picture of the one Body and its many members with different functions and gifts.

#7 *dig in!*

a. Read **Romans 12:4–8** and write out the gift list. We each have unique and specific opportunities (using our treasures, time, and talents) that fall within these many broad gifts, given according to His grace. In the space below, write one or more of the Romans 12 gifts that speaks to you, based on your responses when asked to *Take a Bite* above.

b. Pray, ponder, and discuss how you may use these gifts. Share ideas with others in your group. Get specific. For example, if your gift is leading, where does or could that take place? In what capacity? For and with whom?

What about gifts and talents you've been afraid to use? Don't let them sit on the shelf; resist the notion that they should be saved up or stored. When you or others recognize a gift you have, ask God how He'd like you to use that gift *now*!

- You think of the person you've noticed who needs help putting food on the table, and you are a generous giver. Step out. Don't wait.

- Or maybe you have a friend or family member who needs encouragement and you are a good listener. Go to her now. Pray *for* her and offer to pray *with* her.

- The church is looking for volunteers to teach, and you love sharing God's Word. Don't be afraid to give teaching a try.

- A short-term mission opportunity has just been announced, and the team is looking for another person to serve. You love a challenge, and serving is right up your alley. Inquire!

Unlike chocolate with its short shelf life, our saved or stored-up God-given gifts won't appear to spoil. But if we don't use them, they cannot benefit others. People would miss out on the rich blessings and grace of God they could receive through us. May we, as members of the Body of Christ, serve others, give generously, and reach out in His name using our God-given gifts! To Him be the glory!

Living a Chocolate Life, we use God's good gifts!

PRAYER

Sweet Supplication

Dear God, please forgive me for often storing up and saving Your good and abundant gifts, for failing to use them for Your purposes. Give me the desire to grow in Your Word and in the unity of faith as a member—a vital ingredient—of the Body of Christ. Show me how and where I may use my many gifts today for the benefit of others and for Your glory. In Jesus' precious name. Amen.

✄ TAKE A BITE

Think about the many treasures you possess and how you can share them in the name of Christ to help others and to show His love. What needs have been brought to your attention? How and where can you provide these God-given treasures for others near you? far away?

✄ TAKE A BITE

When and where have you set aside, saved up, or stored some of God's gifts, not using them as you know you should?

Triple Chocolate Rocky Road Brownie Pizza

12 oz. (2 c.) milk chocolate chips, divided
¾ c. unsweetened baking cocoa
2 c. mini marshmallows, divided

1⅓ c. flour	2 c. sugar
1 tsp. baking powder	½ c. coarsely chopped nuts
½ tsp. salt	¾ c. white chocolate chips
⅔ c. vegetable oil	1 tbsp. butter
4 eggs, slightly beaten	2 tsp. vanilla

Preheat oven to 350 degrees. Cut parchment paper to fit a 15-inch round pizza pan or pizza stone. Combine flour, sugar, cocoa, baking powder, and salt. Set aside. Combine oil, eggs, and vanilla; add to dry ingredients. Mix in 1 c. chocolate chips and 1 c. marshmallows. Do not overmix. Spread batter in prepared pan or on pizza stone. Sprinkle remaining 1 c. chocolate chips, 1 c. marshmallows, and chopped nuts over the top. Bake 20 to 25 minutes; let cool. Melt white chocolate chips and butter in saucepan over low heat. Drizzle over cooled pizza. Let set. Slice and serve. *As you savor each bite, marvel at how every vital ingredient worked together to create the whole pizza!*

Your *Chocolate Personality!*

As God continues to reveal to you the unique and amazing gifts He has given you for the good of others and for His glory, consider how your personality plays into the expression and use of your gifts. Are you the nut-filled variety? a cherry cordial, perhaps? a chewy caramel or a rich truffle? As we consider the personality traits with which God has filled us, we can better understand and fulfill the purposes He has for us, using those unique traits to share His love with others. While the following is not an actual personality test, it does provide a glimpse of primary personality types, *chocolate style,* for you to examine. Circle those that apply to you most, and discuss all, as they may apply in lesser ways. (You may be "filled" with a little of each of these, but one or two will likely dominate.) Ask for input from each woman in your group and from others who know you well.

Nut-Filled = Industrious; Worker Like the busy squirrel that stores food for the winter by filling trees with nuts, this not-so-nutty personality works diligently and efficiently behind the scenes; she gets the job done. She is organized and pays attention to detail too.

Cherry Cordial = Loyal; Pleaser Open this special chocolate to find a big red heart (cherry). This tenderhearted personality is always thinking of others, loves to please, and would give the shirt off her back if someone needed it. You can count on her in times of need.

Caramel-Filled = Outgoing; Communicator Like a thick, chewy, caramel-filled chocolate (the kind that you have to chew and chew), this personality is always moving her mouth to communicate freely and lovingly toward everyone around her. Bubbly and extroverted, she loves the company of others.

Dark Truffle–Filled = Motivational; Leader The strong, bold flavor of a dark chocolate truffle makes this candy the perfect match for this dominant personality. Bite into the center and your taste buds wake up and pay attention. Through her words and actions, and by her example, she leads others well.

SESSION 8 · SWEET SURRENDER

A CHOCOLATE SAMPLER

Check all that apply to you, and then discuss as a group:

☑ *You live a sweet, chocolaty life as you use the good gifts God has given you. (Share a nugget of knowledge you gained from the last session and enjoy a Memory Morsel moment.)*

☑ *You surrender regularly to the sweet call of your favorite chocolate creation.*

☑ *You find chocolate _____ irresistible. (Fill in the blank with your favorite chocolate creation.)*

☑ *Your car brakes for the nearest ice-cream shop or bakery.*

☑ *When someone says, "That was a piece of cake," your mouth begins to water.*

☑ *You live a chocolate life of sweet surrender to your Savior. (Read on . . .)*

MEMORY MORSEL

"For it is God who works in you, both to will and to work for His good pleasure." Philippians 2:13

Sweet Surrender

My little white flag just went up. Do you see it? I'm waving it back and forth in front of you. I have held out long enough, and finally, I surrender. I give up. You win. All my resistance is gone. I am no match for you, you irresistible *Melt-in-Your-Mouth Chocolate-Frosted Brownie.* (If you've begun to salivate just hearing the name, don't worry. The recipe follows this session.) I surrender all my willpower, all my diet plans, and I run toward you with fork in hand. Ah, but it is a sweet surrender! *Mmm, delicious!*

I surrender to chocolate of any form, flavor, or variety when it is offered. And when I start, I can't stop! *Just one, thank you. . . . Okay, just one more. . . . Oh, no! I can't believe I ate the whole pan*—again! Why can't I resist?

I know what I want to do: take a little bite to tickle my taste buds, delight in the finest of treats, and enjoy a morsel of chocolate paradise. The first bite, after all, is the most satisfying, pleasing my chocolate-loving palate with a taste sensation that isn't as strong with subsequent bites. Chocolate is good in moderation, so why do I keep digging in? I know what I *don't* want to do: overindulge.

We all have weaknesses, areas of strongest temptation and feeblest resistance against which we cannot stand on our own. Maybe we surrender to gossip or gluttony. Perhaps we give in to peer pressure, envy, or greed. Maybe we struggle with an addiction to something that hurts us and those we love. And what about overindulgence? While some of us may not struggle with excess consumption of chocolate, what about overspending, excessive online gaming, overworking, or other areas of vulnerability?

TAKE A BITE

To what seemingly irresistible weaknesses or areas of temptation do you find yourself yielding or surrendering? Are there areas of overindulgence in which you struggle?

#1 *dig in!*

In every area of our lives, we want to have self-control and vigilance. Instead we are often self-indulgent and unable to resist—chocolate and many other things. Read **1 Peter 5:8–9** for a warning, instruction, and reassurance for believers. Based on these verses, what are some ways the devil seeks to harm us? How can we resist him? (See also **Ephesians 6:10–18** for further warning and detailed instruction.)

Our sins separate us from God and the relationship He desires with us. Even so, He loves us through our binges, overindulgences, and lapses of self-control. These were nailed to the cross with Christ, and His death and resurrection give us final victory over them, restoring our relationship with the Father. (See **Colossians 2:13–15**.) We need not fear the one who threatens to devour us. We humbly submit to our Savior and walk in His Word, where the Holy Spirit fills us with power to not only resist the devil, who flees (**James 4:7**), but also to receive reassurance and strength in our new life in Christ, firm in our faith.

#2 *dig in!*

In **Ephesians 4:17–32,** the apostle Paul teaches about the new life we have in Christ, as opposed to the former way of life devoid of faith. He contrasts the *old self* with the *new self.* By God's grace through faith in Christ, we surrender to Him; we put off the old and put on the new. We've been renewed in our Baptism *and* we are continually being renewed daily by the Spirit's work in us. Read this passage and make two lists, one that defines the *old self,* and the other that defines the *new self,* our new life, one in which we are created in God's likeness.

We know the truth is in Jesus (**v. 21**). Chosen and changed by Him, we don't want to be greedy, dishonest, or slanderous. We want *nothing* to do with the old self! Yet as we look at these lists, too often we see where we have sinned, have fallen for former ways, have failed to resist temptation, have surrendered to our human nature. Rest assured that you can trust the Spirit's saving work in your Baptism and through the Word. The One who redeemed you and fills you with the desire to be like Christ is also transforming you in His likeness. (Remember the moldable masterpiece of Session 6?) Like the psalmist, we can cry out to God with a repentant heart, knowing His grace covers us as He gives us the strength to live our new lives in Christ, surrendered to Him.

#3 dig in!

The Lord knows your heart and your thoughts. He knows the ways in which you struggle. Take them to the Lord, praying **Psalm 139:23–24,** either alone or aloud as a group. Following your prayer time, turn to **2 Corinthians 12:9–10.** The apostle Paul struggled with a specific area of weakness. We all do. What does God have to say about our weakness and His power? How can knowing this help as you consider the struggles in which you all too often surrender?

Remember the little white flag of surrender? Perhaps we can apply the words of my chocolaty surrender story as we acknowledge that God's power is made perfect in our weakness. In His strength, we respond to Him, "We surrender!" *We give up.* We give up all our feeble attempts to be strong enough on our own, all our futile efforts to do good things by our own strength. "*You win, God!* You won salvation for us when You defeated sin, death, and the devil. Because You win, You give us eternal life in Christ! *All our resistance is gone.* Through the power of the Spirit, we no longer resist Your lead, but gladly follow. In our sin, *we are no match for You* in Your holiness, but You took away our sin and made us holy in Christ! *We surrender all* our evil thoughts and ways to Your perfect ones. Jesus, *You run toward us* with outstretched arms. Filled with Your Spirit, we yield to Your loving touch. Truly, this is sweet, *sweet surrender!*"

I Can't Wait!

I am having a chocolate craving *now!* I can't wait! Hurry, pull in to the nearest chocolate shop or bakery. The closest gas station will do. What? There's a line at checkout? Does this mean I have to *wait* for what I want *right now?*

At home, I place the candy dish strategically on the path between the kitchen and living room. I grab a handful as I pass by (both ways). What? The candy dish is empty? I have to *wait* to purchase more? But I want it *now!* I can't wait!

Do any of my need-it-*now* chocolate cravings really provide the gratification I seek? Or do they merely offer careless calories that I could have saved for something sensational later, like a special chocolate dessert this weekend or a trip to the ice-cream shop tomorrow?

How often are we impatient in life, going for instant gratification instead of waiting for something better? Our culture says to grab hold of whatever we crave *now.* Overspend now; concern yourself with credit card payment later. Overeat now; worry about indigestion later. Do what feels good now; lose sleep over the consequences later. Instant gratification rules, regardless of the results.

CHOCOLATE FUN FACT
Did you know that solid chocolate, the kind that graces our candy dishes today, didn't exist until the middle of the nineteenth century? For hundreds of years, chocolate was consumed only as a bitter beverage. Eventually sugar was added for a sweet drink. Finally, in the 1850s, an Englishman experimented by adding more cocoa butter instead of water and created the first solid chocolate.

#4 *dig in!*

While the culture competes for our attention, God's Word gently redirects us to the place of our first priority. Read **Matthew 6:33** and **Colossians 3:1–2**, looking also at the context surrounding them. What is the Lord telling us to seek first, to set our minds on? As you read these words, consider how God may be gently redirecting you in specific ways. Share and discuss.

Our Savior knew His purpose, the path to our salvation set before Him by the Father, but He patiently waited for God's perfect timing. Many times Jesus told His followers that His time had not yet come (see **John 7:6–8**). With His mind on things above, Jesus obediently endured the cross and won salvation for us at just the right time.

#5 *dig in!*

The passages that follow refer to God's perfect timing in fulfilling His plan for our salvation. What do we learn about the "right time" or the "fullness of time"? Look to these passages for unique descriptions, telling us when, how, and for whom.

- Romans 5:6–8

- Galatians 4:4–5

- Ephesians 1:7–10

God's gift of faith enables us to surrender to Him—to set our minds on things above—and the desire for instant gratification fades. Empowered by the Holy Spirit, we patiently wait in eager anticipation for the Lord Jesus Christ to come again and take us home to heaven. **"But our citizenship is in heaven, and from it we await a Savior, the Lord Jesus Christ" (Philippians 3:20).** He has something far better than this world offers, and it is well worth the wait!

A Piece of Cake

When a friend says, "That was a piece of cake!" we know she accomplished something with ease. This fun expression suggests the effortless achievement of swallowing a slice of sweet dessert, another *sweet surrender*!

Oddly enough, the familiar phrase "a piece of cake" did not originate in a bakery, but in the Royal Air Force in the late 1930s. It was used to refer to an easily accomplished mission, "a piece of cake." (And surely those pilots were thinking of *chocolate* cake, weren't they?!)

What are our missions in life? Are they each a piece of cake? A few are, perhaps, but so often we wish that our many arduous tasks, responsibilities, and obligations were a little easier—tasks such as working, raising a family, managing relationships, and more. Wouldn't it be great if accomplishing all our goals were as easy as sitting and savoring a fat slice of *Extravagant Chocolate Three-Layer Cake?* (Yum! See Session 1.)

TAKE A BITE
What do you see as your missions in life right now? Which ones, if any, are a *piece of cake*? What about the others?

TAKE ANOTHER BITE
Where do you see examples of the desire and perceived need for instant gratification in the culture around you? in yourself?

#6 *dig in!*

God has a mission for us. Explore what that mission includes as you look up the following verses. Jot them down here and discuss together with your group: Is this mission a piece of cake?

- 1 Peter 1:15

- Luke 10:27

- Matthew 5:44

- Ephesians 4:32

Ouch! This mission is *not* a piece of cake. In fact, our sinfulness makes it impossible. On our own, we are incapable of holiness or righteousness, of love or forgiveness. It is impossible for us to save ourselves from our sin. But what is impossible for us is possible with God! **"Jesus . . . said, 'With man this is impossible, but with God all things are possible'" (Matthew 19:26).**

See the beautiful sunrise God just painted across the horizon? That was a piece of cake for Him! Mountains moved? A breeze. Peace provided in the midst of strife? A cinch. Prayers answered? Yes, another piece of cake.

But what about the mission that sent Christ to Calvary? It wasn't a piece of cake for God to send His perfect Son to bear the filthy sins of the whole world on the cross. Yet we know that all things are possible with God in His great mercy and love. Jesus' mission saved us from sin, death, and eternal condemnation. His mission for our salvation was complete, as Jesus' resurrection assures us. Filling us with His Spirit, He provides the strength and the ability to accomplish every task in our lives that is not a piece of cake, as well as those that are.

#7 *dig in!*

a. God has given us our ultimate mission, and by His grace through faith, we surrender our lives to the Lord for His purpose. Check out **2 Corinthians 5:20** and **Galatians 5:13–14** for illustrations of what this mission (our purpose!) looks like.

b. Our mission would be impossible on our own. Praise God we're not on our own! **"For it is God who works in you, both to will and to work for His good pleasure" (Philippians 2:13).** *(Memory Morsel)* Not only does our Lord work in us and through us, enabling us to accomplish His mission, but there's more! Read **Ephesians 3:20–21**. Whose power is at work within us? What's our role? And what does God do with our mission work?

A chocolate life is a life of *sweet surrender*! In everything we do, we acknowledge Him as Lord of our lives, and He directs our paths **(Proverbs 3:6).** We yield to His perfect plan and timing as we wait for Christ's return. Submitting to Him, we can only imagine the amazing mission ahead as the Spirit works in us, fulfilling His purposes according to His perfect will.

A Chocolate Life is a life of sweet surrender to the Lord!

Sweet Supplication

Lord, I surrender my ways to You. Work in me and through me to do Your will, for Your purposes and for Your good pleasure. Thank You for loving me in my weaknesses, that You were willing to die for me, giving me final victory over them and eternal life with You! Give me Your power to stand firm in faith. Lord Jesus, I can't wait for You to come again. Through Your Spirit, set my mind on things above. Help me to wait patiently for Your perfect timing and Your perfect plans. Lord, I know that nothing is impossible for You! Give me Your strength for the mission You have for me. In Jesus' name I pray. Amen.

CHOCOTIVITY

Sweet Surrender Chocolate Buffet

Have each woman in your Bible study choose and bake a recipe from one of these eight chocolaty sessions and bring them together for a time of *sweet surrender*. (If someone isn't able to bake, she could choose, instead, to bring samples of her favorite chocolates.) With a plentiful assortment of chocolate pleasures, this may be a great time to invite other women or to turn the buffet into a family event. Provide plates, napkins, forks, and beverages. Label each chocolate treat and be prepared to share a nugget of God's truth, as each delicacy relates to a sumptuous chocolate session. If inviting guests, consider sending them home with a thanks-for-coming gift. Fun gift ideas may include a *Living a Chocolate Life* devotion book attached to one of several related items, like a box of chocolates, a hot cocoa packet tucked in a mug, an extra-large chocolate bar, an assortment of chocolate-scented candles or spa products, or a chocolate baking basket, complete with recipes and ingredients.

Melt-in-Your-Mouth Chocolate-Frosted Brownies

These chocolate-frosted brownies don't look unusual; their secret lies in the runny batter, which bakes quickly at a high temperature. The result: irresistible, melt-in-your-mouth, chocolate perfection! It's a *sweet surrender*!

2 c. flour	2 c. sugar
1 c. (2 sticks) butter	1 c. water
¼ c. unsweetened baking cocoa	½ c. buttermilk
2 eggs	1 tsp. baking soda
1 tsp. vanilla	

Preheat oven to 400 degrees. Thoroughly grease an 11 x 17-inch pan. Mix flour and sugar in a bowl; set aside. In a saucepan, combine butter, water, and cocoa. Heat to boiling, stirring constantly, then pour over the dry mixture and blend well. Add buttermilk, eggs, baking soda, and vanilla. Mix well with hand mixer, then pour into prepared pan. Bake 20 minutes. While brownies are baking, prepare the frosting.

Frosting

½ c. (1 stick) butter	¼ c. milk
3½ c. powdered sugar	1 tsp. vanilla
3 tbsp. unsweetened baking cocoa	

In a saucepan, combine butter, cocoa, and milk; heat to boiling, stirring constantly. Remove from heat; blend in powdered sugar and vanilla until frosting is smooth. Pour warm frosting over brownies while brownies are also still warm.

Wrapped in His Grace

Are you *living a chocolate life*? The answer is "Yes! By the *grace* of God!" While many fine ingredients can be found that add taste and texture to a recipe for a chocolate-rich life, they all hinge on one vital ingredient: *grace.* God's sweet, extravagant grace!

By His grace, we live *a chocolate life* in so many ways, as we've studied during all eight sessions. Empowered by the Holy Spirit, we live our lives in joyful response to the new life God gives us in Christ.

When you opened this study to Session 1, you savored in your imagination an extravagant morsel of rare, foil-wrapped chocolate. God's grace is no imagined extravagance. It's real and it's eternal—larger and more lavish than a lifetime supply of the most perfect, delicate chocolate. Dear sister, savor His saving grace in Christ!

God has the final word on grace. Will you pray with me the final words of Scripture? **"The grace of the Lord Jesus be with all. Amen" (Revelation 22:21).**

Session 1

#1 (Wording of explanation will vary.) We receive forgiveness of our sins and eternal life through Christ's perfect atoning sacrifice, by the shedding of His blood, His death on the cross. He died that we can live!

   a. In the original Greek language of the New Testament, the word for "redemption" *(apolytrosis)* means literally "to buy back" a slave or captive, to set the person free. Christ's life was the price paid to buy back sinners from captivity to our trespasses.

   b. To "lavish" is to give generously, in abundance. Examples may include pouring hot fudge liberally over a loved one's sundae until the ice cream is covered and fudge runs down the sides of the dish; or giving someone a most extravagant, expensive chocolate gift. God's grace is lavished upon us; the verse even speaks to the *riches* of His grace. The measure of our Savior's mercy and grace is rich, overflowing, extravagant!

#2 He is rich in mercy; He has great love for us and kindness toward us in Christ. He shows us the immeasurable riches of His grace: He made us alive together with Christ, even when we were dead in our sins, raising us up with Him and seating us with Him in the heavenly places—securing for us a place in heaven for eternity with Him.

#3 We first learn of Saul in **Acts 7**, at the stoning of Stephen, the first Christian martyr. Saul was not only present but also giving his approval at the stoning. Similarly, in **Acts 26**, Paul admits that he cast his vote against those who were being stoned; both are indications that Saul was a Pharisee (Jewish religious leader) with great authority, leading the charge as an enemy of the cross of Christ. We are reminded of the extent of God's limitless grace, that He would forgive and choose even Saul; and that He forgives and chooses even you and me.

#4 Discussion will vary. Christ speaks to Saul from heaven in a blinding light. He speaks also to a disciple named Ananias in a vision, giving the grace-filled message that Saul (of all people!) is His chosen instrument. Though afraid, Ananias responds in obedience, and by God's power, restores Saul's sight. Saul is immediately baptized and filled with the Holy Spirit.

#5 He humbly admits he is unworthy to be called an apostle because he persecuted the Church; he refers to himself as "the least of the apostles." He recognizes that it is solely by God's grace that he has been chosen to carry the Good News to the world; it's the grace of God enabling him to work as he does. It's by His grace that we, too, are chosen to follow Him, and it's the grace of God, working through the Holy Spirit, that enables us to work as we do.

#6 *a*. Answers will vary as women share areas of brokenness. More possibilities include: worry, greed, hate, envy, sexual immorality, idolatry, jealousy, anger, addictions.

   ***b*.** Whether confessing aloud or silently, give and receive reassurance that your sins are forgiven. You are healed—covered by the riches of God's grace in Christ.

#7 *a*. "He himself bore our sins in His body on the tree, that we might die to sin and live to righteousness. By His wounds you have been healed" (1 Peter 2:24).

   ***b*.** Because Christ bore our sins, dying in our place ("wounded for our transgressions"), we as believers are dead to sin and live new lives; we are made righteous (*justified*, made right with God) through Christ by faith. Though, like Paul, we struggle with sin, it no longer holds us captive. We are healed. We have victory and eternal life in Christ!

ANSWERS TO DIG IN! QUESTIONS

Session 2

#1 *a*. Be kind and tenderhearted; forgive one another; be imitators of God; walk in love. (Personalization will be unique to each person.)

   ***b*.** To imitate God is to live a chocolate-rich life of grace and love, forgiving undeserving sinners as He forgave us (who are also undeserving sinners) through Christ's cross, and walking in sacrificial love—the kind of love Christ has for us. The Greek word used here for "*walk*" (*stoicheo*) means "be in line with" or "keep in step with." As imitators, we keep in step with the One we desire to emulate. We are able to do any of this only because of what He first did for us, through the power of the Holy Spirit!

#2 It was a pleasing aroma to the Lord in that He accepted the sacrifice, offered up through the priests by repentant sinners, and He provided forgiveness through it. **Leviticus 1:4** explained that the sacrifice **"shall be accepted for [the sinner] to make atonement for him,"** though the sacrifice was imperfect and incomplete, which necessitated repeated regular offerings.

#3 *a.* Picture a victorious army proclaiming triumph over the enemy as they march through a city in triumphal procession. In Christ, we have victory over the ultimate enemies of sin, death, and the devil.

   b. The fragrant offering of Christ's sacrifice on the cross and the resulting salvation in Him is the heart of the message that we share, as we follow Him triumphantly and His fragrance flows through us. This message of forgiveness is a sweet aroma for all who believe.

#4 We have all sinned, but we are justified (saved) freely, not by our own works, but by His grace as a gift through Christ's redemption. We have access to His grace by faith, and we rejoice because we have the promise of eternal life; our hope is in Him! The Holy Spirit has been **"poured out on us richly" (Titus 3:6)**, giving us new life in our Baptism, a means by which we receive His grace. (Discussion of opportunities will vary.)

#5 Put on: a compassionate heart, kindness, humility, meekness, patience, forgiveness, and love (surrounding the others in the visual of a heart, as it "binds everything together in perfect harmony").

#6 The list includes, in part: contributing to other believers' needs; showing hospitality; blessing people who persecute you; crying with others as they cry; living peaceably with everyone; overcoming evil with good. (Pause to talk about each, including those not mentioned here, as time allows. Discussion of opportunities will vary.)

#7 *a.* We should fill our speech with praise and kind words. Our talk is to be wholesome, our words full of grace-filled flavor as we speak the truth in love.

   b. Salt-seasoned speech, wise conversation, not only pleases God and builds up fellow believers, but also perks up the ears of others who listen, especially "outsiders," those whom we may have the opportunity to impact for Christ.

Session 3

#1 a. They can't satisfy our spiritual hunger because they offer *less* than what we really need. When we use the things of this world in an attempt to satiate emotional and spiritual needs (a hole they were never meant to fill), they become unhealthy. Because they are inadequate substitutes, they leave us malnourished and longing for more.

b. Food is a word picture Isaiah uses to warn against false teaching ("that which is not bread") and chasing after idols and other things that cannot satisfy us spiritually. Similarly, we should not chase after the things of this world in an attempt to fill our spiritual needs that can only be filled by the Lord. The rich food of God's Word is the way in which our spiritual hunger can be satisfied. We "eat what is good" as we listen and learn from Him by the Holy Spirit's work and as we receive His life-giving gifts.

#2 a. Jesus broke the barrier of hostility between Jews and Samaritans by speaking to her, but greater than that, by His request, He was reaching out to this woman with His saving grace and love. He told her that if she only knew who it was asking her for a drink, that *she* would be asking *Him*. And He would give her "living water"—the gift of God by the power of the Holy Spirit. Salvation in Christ. Eternal life. The only thing that satisfies continually, and only Jesus can give it. Only He can fully satisfy.

b. Jesus revealed that He knew about her previous five husbands and the man she was living with now. He was leading her to a recognition of her sin while revealing to her that He knew everything about her. She had likely been hurt and rejected repeatedly as she sought to be filled by unhealthy relationships in her unsuccessful attempts to find satisfaction for what she really needed. Jesus then revealed to her that He was the Messiah—the Christ. She knew and believed the prophecies that told of the coming Messiah, and He stood before her now.

c. She ran to the townspeople and told them, **"Come, see a man who told me all that I ever did. Can this be the Christ?" (v. 29).** The people actually listened to her, and many believed in Jesus because of her testimony **(v. 39)!** God's grace overflows in us. Like the Samaritan woman, we want to shout His salvation to the world in response to what He has done for us.

#3 *a.* **Psalm 63:1–5; 90:14:** He satisfies *(your name)* with His steadfast love, which is better than life **(63:3). Psalm 103:1–5:** He forgives your sin, heals your diseases, and redeems your life from the grave. He crowns you with His love and mercy. He satisfies you with good, renewing your strength. **Psalm 145:15–16:** He provides for all of your needs, and He satisfies your desires. (Personalization will be unique to each person.)

b. In response, we rejoice; we can be glad every day of our lives. With our mouths and with all that is in us, we praise Him. We look to Him for all our provision as He satisfies completely. (Personalize in prayer.)

#4 Jeremiah 31:3: He *loves* _____ *(insert your name)* with an everlasting love and is continually faithful to _____. **Romans 8:38–39:** Absolutely nothing can separate _____ from His love in Christ! **Ephesians 3:16–19:** By the power of His Spirit in _____, Christ dwells in _____'s heart through faith, that _____ may have strength to comprehend how great His love is for _____, which surpasses knowledge! **1 John 4:9–10:** In God's love for _____, He sent His Son to die in _____'s place, that _____ may have eternal life in Him.

#5 *Peace* is not merely "lack of war," as the world often defines it. We receive true peace with God through faith in Christ, who reconciled us with the Father by His saving work on the cross **(Romans 5:1)**. The extent of God's loving care for us and His provision of peace are beyond our comprehension, but we can call out to God with our requests, and He fills us with peace, guarding our hearts and minds in Christ, even in the midst of trials, when we would otherwise be anxious, troubled, or afraid **(Philippians 4:6–7)**.

#6 2 Corinthians 1:3–4: As we are *comforted* in our affliction, God's strength enables us to comfort others in theirs, with the same comfort we have been given. *Can chocolate do all that?!* **2 Thessalonians 2:16–17:** He comforts our hearts as He guides us in our words and work. (Shared stories of comfort, received and given, will be unique to each person.)

#7 *Security:* He rescues us and makes our steps secure. We are safe in the care of our Strong Tower. *Strength:* He provides strength when we are weak, renewing our strength as we hope in Him. We are strengthened by His power for endurance and patience. *Contentment:* By Christ's strength, we are able to learn contentment in every circumstance, confident of His provision for all our needs. (Personalization will be unique to each person.)

ANSWERS TO DIG IN! QUESTIONS

Session 4

#1 Genesis 17:1–8, 15–16: God promises to Abraham that He will establish an everlasting covenant with him; that Abraham will be the father of a multitude of nations; that God will be their God and they will be His chosen people. And He will begin by miraculously giving Abraham and his wife a son in their old age. This was fulfilled in **21:1–2.** God promises to give Abraham's descendants the land of Canaan (which will come to be known as "the Promised Land"). **Exodus 3:7–8, 16–17:** Centuries later, God promises Moses that He will deliver His people from captivity in Egypt to this Promised Land. **Joshua 21:43–45:** Joshua proclaims God's fulfilled promises, which have been known for generations and are now realized, as His people have conquered the Promised Land by God's mighty hand. (Notice Joshua's words concerning *all* of God's promises in **v. 45.**)

#2 God promises to David (**Psalm 89:3–4**) that He will have a descendant on the throne forever. Similarly, He speaks through the prophet Isaiah about the Child to be born from David's line, ascribing titles for Him (**Isaiah 9:6–7**) that can only be fully realized in the messianic King who will rule His kingdom eternally with *justice and righteousness* (see **Psalm 89:14**). He describes in detail through Isaiah how Christ will suffer, take all our sorrows, griefs, and sins upon Himself, and pour out His life for us, dying in our place and interceding for us to the Father, providing for us eternal healing and peace (**Isaiah 53:3–6**). God foretells through **Jeremiah** that He will fulfill His promise of the Messiah—"a righteous Branch" (**33:15**)—through David's descendants, again speaking of a rule of *justice and righteousness.* Only Jesus, the sinless Son of God, can provide complete and lasting justice; He declares us just and covers us with His righteousness through forgiveness at the cross and new life in His name!

#3 God's promise to Abraham came by God's grace through faith, and not by the Law. By faith, *we* are Abraham's offspring, recipients of the promise of salvation, chosen in Christ! By faith, Abraham believed God's promises that he would be the father of many nations, and that he and his wife would have a son. (Recall **Genesis 17** from #1.) By the same faith, we believe in God who raised His Son, Jesus, from the dead, and by that faith, we have eternal life. Righteousness by faith will be "counted to us" as it was to Abraham.

#4 Sink your teeth into these delightful verses that speak of God's creation and His salvation in Christ!

#5 *Presence:* The Lord is with you always and will never leave you. *Protection:* He is your fortress, help, and shield, in whom you can take refuge. He protects you day and night from evil and all harm. *Provision:* The Lord knows your needs and richly provides for you; He is the giver of every good and perfect gift. *Purpose:* You were created in Christ to do the good work planned for you, even as He has equipped you and works in you that you may do His will.

#6 Answers will vary and may include: He is personally *present* in the Word and the Sacraments; His hand of *protection* is upon you, spiritually and physically, in each situation; His *provision* is there for you when you need it most, in everything from unexpected funds to a new friend; His *purpose* is revealed as doors open to share Christ's love with someone or to help another in need.

#7 *a.* The Lord has promised us love and salvation (**Psalm 119:41**), grace (**v. 58**), and comfort (v. **76**) from His love; He promises that He will uphold you (**v. 116**), keep steady your steps (**v. 133**), and give you redemption and life (**v. 154**).

   b. Personalized promises, taken to the Lord in prayer, will be unique to each person.

ANSWERS TO DIG IN! QUESTIONS

Session 5

#1 *a.* Shortcuts just don't cut it. But in our sin, we cannot love perfectly, as His Law (summed up in **Mark 12:30–31**) commands. He fulfilled the Law perfectly for us, offers us forgiveness, and works in us now, enabling us to give our best.

   b. In Mark 12:30–31, Jesus makes His point powerfully as He separates and stresses "all" repeatedly, signifying every part of us in our love for the Lord. Colossians 3:23–24 tells us we're to work heartily, remembering that even as we serve another, we are serving Christ. Our reward is our inheritance in heaven—eternal life! Knowing this makes all the difference, enabling us to persevere when the work is menial or difficult, or when those we serve are unfair or even cruel.

#2 **"And there is salvation in no one else, for there is no other name under heaven given among men by which we must be saved" (Acts 4:12).** The only way of salvation, the only way to the Father in heaven, is through faith in Christ Jesus, His Son.

#3 Acts 20:29–30: False teachers—"fierce wolves"—will come in, along with people already among you, and they will twist words, corrupting the Gospel, to pull believers away. **2 Corinthians 11:13–15:** Deceivers will disguise themselves as apostles. Like Satan, his servants also disguise themselves so as to deceive people. **Galatians 1:6–9:** Some among you want to distort the Gospel of Christ; they will be accursed. **2 Peter 2:1–3:** False teachers among you will secretly bring in false teachings, even denying Christ as Savior, and many will follow them; "the way of truth will be blasphemed" (v. 2), and people will be exploited with the false teachers' lies.

#4 Unlike some others Paul visited, the Bereans eagerly received the Word as he shared it; they were open to listening. They tested everything they were hearing against the Old Testament Scriptures, which had promised and prophesied a Messiah was coming, to make sure Paul's claims were really true: that Jesus had perfectly fulfilled the prophecies and God's promise of a Savior. Having carefully examined the Scriptures, **"many of them therefore believed" (v. 12),** a testimony to the truth of Paul's Gospel message.

#5 Psalm 119:9–16: By memorizing His Word, it is "stored up," enabling us to act upon it. (Memory Morsels!) By learning His Word, speaking it, delighting in it, and meditating on it as we study, we keep our eyes on His ways. His Spirit enables us to guard and live our lives by His Word. **Colossians 3:16:** His Word lives and grows in us as we teach and correct one another in God's wisdom, as the Word is spoken or sung with thanksgiving to Him!

#6 a. Those who confess Jesus as God in the flesh have the Spirit of God in them; those who do not confess Jesus are not of God and are doing the work of the devil—they have in them "the spirit of the antichrist" (**1 John 4:3**).

  b. We have overcome them through faith in Christ. We have victory in Him! Jesus lives in all who believe, and by His death and resurrection, He has conquered not only sin and death, but the devil too. Our Savior is incomparably greater and stronger than the devil and the evil spirits who try to deceive us.

#7 *a*. We prepare the same way we stand strong in the one true faith, so that we will not be deceived by imitation claims: we go to God's Word! Do not let your lack of Bible knowledge keep you from witnessing your faith, but continue to grow in the Word, trusting the Holy Spirit's work in and through you, as you learn and as you make a defense to those who ask.

   b. Concerning the first part of the verse, our witness for Christ begins with our own faith walk, our belief in Christ as Lord and Savior! We honor Him as holy as we trust Him for strength to lead a God-pleasing life that glorifies Him and serves as a witness to an unbelieving world. Concerning the last part of the verse, our answer should always be given in love, even when facing opposition from unbelievers. Respectfully listen to them and be gentle with them, even as they doubt or question, all while sharing the truth in love.

ANSWERS TO DIG IN! QUESTIONS

Session 6

#1 Your Rescuer sees you, hears your cries, and is near. He delivers you out of all your troubles and saves you. Maybe you won't receive rescue from a specific struggle today or even tomorrow, but you can trust His care over you and His deliverance of you. He has already rescued and delivered you out of your greatest trouble, saving you from your sin.

#2 Deuteronomy 31:8: In every circumstance, He goes before you *and* He is with you; He will never leave you, so you don't need to be afraid! **Psalm 73:23:** He holds you by the hand. **Isaiah 43:1:** The Creator who formed you has redeemed you; He calls you by your name—you are His! **Zephaniah 3:17:** He is mighty to save you, and He not only rejoices over you, but also quiets and calms you with His love.

#3 *a*. God says it's a "gracious thing" (**1 Peter 2:19**) in His sight—it's commendable to Him—when we endure while suffering for doing good, for standing strong in our faith and honoring Christ in our words and work, regardless of the consequences. Christ suffered to save us, and by His grace, we "follow in His steps" (**v. 21**). Though our sufferings are incomparably smaller than His, we share in His sufferings in trials that test our faith, through which God is strengthening us.

b. Jesus did not retaliate but trusted God to judge fairly. By His strength, we can love our enemies and pray for those who persecute us (see **Matthew 5:44**). We can *rejoice* that we get to share in His suffering, because His glory is revealed through us when others receive the Good News of Jesus that we bring. We are blessed as we are being insulted and persecuted because God is with us, empowering us by His Spirit to stand up under it.

#4 Psalm 57:2: You can cry out to God who fulfills His purpose for you! **Proverbs 19:21:** While you may have many plans in mind, it's God's purpose that will stand. **Isaiah 55:8–9:** His ways and His thoughts are different and better (higher) than yours. **Jeremiah 29:11:** He knows the plans He has for you, for your good and not for evil, giving you a future and a hope. (Allow these truths to guide you in prayer.)

#5 *a*. We can respond with joy, trusting that God is producing much through them, using them for our good and His purpose. Christlike qualities include: endurance, character, hope, steadfastness, perfection, and completion. Walk through a past or present trial and recount where you had to *endure* to get through it, recognizing it was God's strength that brought you through, whether you knew it at the time or not. Consider the *character* that developed in you over time and the resultant *hope* you have received in Him, even if the trial continues today. (Specific answers are as unique as each person.)

b. Romans 5:5: By the Holy Spirit's work in our lives, our hope of eternal life in Christ is sure and certain! James 1:2–4: "Steadfastness" refers to patience that we gain through our trials, which leads to "perfection," meaning full maturity in our faith, that we may be "complete" with a strong faith, sure of our salvation and the promise of heaven, the place of perfection.

#6 Romans 8:28 tells us that we who love God (in response to His great love for us!) are called to live and serve for His purpose, and we trust that He is working all things (the good, the bad, and the bitter) together for *good*. As you share this truth from the heart with someone who is suffering or struggling, you may also want to talk about your past experience as it applies to theirs, sharing with honesty and vulnerability how you believe the Lord has or will use it for your good or the good of others.

#7 The Lord speaks from His throne, telling us we will be with Him in His immediate presence forever. He will wipe away all of our tears, and there will be no more death, mourning, crying, or pain. When we look at our every circumstance in light of a perfect eternity with our Savior in heaven, even the most difficult trial is put into perspective. This trial is temporary; heaven is eternal.

ANSWERS TO DIG IN! QUESTIONS

Session 7

#1 *a.* Their role, as they teach and preach from the pure Word of God, is to equip all believers for the work of ministry, to build up the Body of Christ. The purpose is to bring everyone to unity of faith, mature in the knowledge of Christ, so that we won't be deceived or led astray by false teachings or doctrine (see also Session 5). As we grow in faith through the Word, the Holy Spirit works through us, empowering us to share the love of God in Christ through our words and actions in our vocations (in every part of our lives, whatever our calling and career).

b. We grow up in Christ as we grow in the Word, proclaimed and taught in truth and purity of doctrine, and as we work together in unity as one Body, in which Christ is the Head. Filled with His truth and using the unique gifts God has given us, the entire Body of Christ grows and is built up in love, as He works through us!

#2 The two gifts mentioned here involve *speaking* and *serving,* the use of our words and our actions. Using God's many and various gifts to benefit others will involve one, the other, or both! When we speak "oracles" (**1 Peter 4:11**), or words of God, we're sharing His truth with speech that's guided by Scripture. When we serve, we're relying on God's strength. In our words *and* actions, God is glorified through Christ.

#3 There are *varieties*—different kinds—of spiritual gifts, different ways to serve, and different activities/work to be done. But the *same* Spirit produces every one of our gifts. The *same* Lord works through every act of service for His purpose. The *same* God empowers us to use each gift He has given. The vast varieties of spiritual gifts include those that are uniquely shared through you (your combination of gifts and opportunities is *different* from all others'), while all are united by the *same* God who gives them all! (Personalization will be unique to each person.)

#4 Verses 15–16; 19; 20; 25

#5 *a.* Cheerful giving flows out of a heart of willingness and a desire to share. As we grow in faith through the power of the Holy Spirit, our desires begin to change. Where we may have once held tightly to the treasures we possess, we grow to see that they've all come from the Lord's hand (**James 1:17**), and our grip on them loosens. He gives us the ability and desire to cheerfully give the good gifts of our treasures, regardless of their form.

b. "All" speaks of God's full and perfect provision. The Lord richly blesses us with an overflowing measure of His grace, filling us with everything *(all)* that we need, including the desire and capacity for generous giving, so that in *all* we do at *all* times, we will be able to overflow ("abound"!) in *all* our good works, accomplished in His name and by His strength working in us.

#6 These verses encourage us, even exhort us, to "[make] the best use of the time." We make use of the precious time we are given when we conscientiously use our time at work, at leisure, and in every area of our lives for other people. We can pray for God's guidance in every relationship, interaction, and opportunity, as we may be led to listen, help, show care, offer forgiveness, teach, encourage, and share and show our faith!

#7 *a.* Prophecy, service, teaching, exhortation/encouragement, giving, leading, showing mercy

    b. Answers and ideas will vary. Encourage and assist one another as you discuss gifts and specifically where and how you may be called to use them for His purpose and glory.

ANSWERS TO DIG IN! QUESTIONS

Session 8

#1 We are warned that we must be sober-minded (self-controlled) and watchful, ready for Christ's return. Satan, pictured here as a roaring lion, seeks to pounce upon and devour Christians. He wants to harm us any way he can, often wearing us down by preying on our weaknesses or by attempting to take our eyes off the Lord. We resist the devil by God's power working through the Word, which strengthens our faith and prepares us to face temptation. We stand **"firm in [our] faith" (1 Peter 5:9)** that God freely gives!

#2 The *old self* is darkened in understanding, alienated from God, ignorant, hard-hearted, callous, given to sensuality, greedy, impure, corrupt, deceitful. The old self lies, sins in anger (which gives the devil a foothold), steals, speaks corrupt words, and grieves the Holy Spirit (denies God; rejects faith). The old self is filled with bitterness, wrath, anger, clamor, slander, and malice. The *new self* is created in God's likeness, righteous and holy. The new self speaks truth, works honestly in order to share with those in need, and speaks grace-filled words that are appropriate for each occasion—words that build others up. The new self is kind, tenderhearted, and forgiving.

#3 His grace is enough (sufficient!) to cover us in our weakness. Though God's power is already perfect, it is made more obvious and evident in our weakness as we humbly admit our need for His strength and submit to Him, that **"the power of Christ may rest upon [us]" (2 Corinthians 12:9).** We know that as we surrender our every weakness to Him, not only does His grace cover us, but we can even be content in our difficulties, trusting that His power is what gives us strength to stand up in them.

#4 We're called to seek first the kingdom of God, and to set our minds on things above (heavenly things). Maybe the Lord is gently redirecting you if you've been preoccupied primarily with the material desires of this world, worries over finances and provision, and the longing for earthly pleasures that you've placed ahead of your relationship with the Lord. Surrender to the Lord—to His plan, His will, and His timing. (Discussions will vary.)

#5 Romans 5:6–8: In God's perfect timing, He sent His Son to die for us while we were still weak sinners. **Galatians 4:4–5:** He came to us, fully God (God's Son) and fully man (born of woman), that by His perfect sacrifice (fulfilling the Law), we could be adopted by God as His children. **Ephesians 1:7–10:** In the fullness of time, God's purpose to redeem us, to reconcile us to Himself, was revealed in Christ (the answer to the mystery!), the fulfillment of all messianic prophecies.

#6 1 Peter 1:15: He has called us to be holy and righteous before Him. **Luke 10:27:** We are to love Him with all of our being and love others as we love ourselves. **Matthew 5:44:** We are to love our enemies. **Ephesians 4:32:** We are to forgive others as He has forgiven us.

#7 *a.* Our ultimate mission, our purpose, is to spread the Good News of Christ and to serve one another in love! As defined by these verses, we have the humble privilege of representing Jesus as God speaks through us, urging those who are lost to repent of their sins, to be reconciled to Him in Christ Jesus (**2 Corinthians 5:20**). Forgiven in Christ and free from sin's bondage, we are able to serve and love our neighbor (**Galatians 5:13–14**).

   b. Led by the power of the Holy Spirit, we trust and obey the Lord, completing the mission to which He has called us, and He uses it for so much more! He can do through us "far more abundantly" (Ephesians 3:20) than we could ask or imagine!